Every Day the River Changes

FOUR WEEKS DOWN
THE MAGDALENA

Jordan Salama

Catapult  New York

Small portions of this book first appeared, in different form, in essays published in *The New York Times* and *ReVista: Harvard Review of Latin America*.

ISBN: 978-1-64622-044-1

Jacket design by Lexi Earle
Book design by Jordan Koluch
Maps illustrated by Daniel Hasenbos

Library of Congress Control Number: 2021931547

Catapult
1140 Broadway, Suite 706
New York, NY 10001

Printed in the United States of America
1 3 5 7 9 10 8 6 4 2

For my family

CONTENTS

Part Three: Lower Magdalena

EVERY DAY THE RIVER CHANGES

Introduction

IT WAS SUNSET WHEN I SAW THE BOATS.

I was walking close to the water and stopped, letting the waves lap gently against my feet as I stared out toward the horizon. They did not look like regular boats. They looked like submarines, because you could only see the pointed black tips on either end protruding from the swells of the sea. Every evening, reliably, just before twilight, they would curiously jet across the horizon in a single-file line, and I would watch them. Finally, I thought to ask.

"What are those boats for?" I turned to Vismar and Colo, two boys my age whom I'd befriended in this Pacific beach town of Colombia called Ladrilleros.

"Those ones are the fishing boats," Vismar said. He and Colo cackled, as they often did when they heard my Argentine-accented Spanish with an American tinge or when I asked questions that they thought were strange, like how they knew their way around the labyrinth of backwater mangroves like roads or what went on in the jungle-clad mountains that loomed over our heads.

"Why are you laughing?" I asked this time.

"We call them fishing boats, but they only fish during the day."

Colo clarified. "At night, they continue north, to bring the cocaine to Central America."

They cackled again, even louder now. My face turned bright red, and I immediately regretted having asked anything at all. It was 2016, my first time in a foreign country alone. I was nineteen, wary and scared. I had been told to ask questions about anything I wanted but never about the cocaine. Never the guerrillas. That's how you got in trouble in Colombia, people said, by asking too many questions about the wrong things.

I guess Vismar and Colo noticed my discomfort. "Don't worry about it, really," Colo reassured me, and he was being earnest. "Around here, everything's calm." Tranquilo.

I nodded. Colo walked ahead and motioned for me to follow. But then Vismar mumbled something under his breath, and Colo stopped.

They stood very close to each other and whispered things very quickly and incomprehensibly, as if debating whether to tell me something.

"What is it?" I asked nervously.

"No, it's really nothing," Colo said, and they kept whispering. I did not say anything. Finally, after about a minute, they stopped, and Vismar came over to me.

"Well," he said, "there is one thing we think you should know." I looked to my left. The boats had sped away, out of view. To my right, lanky waterfalls poured from volcanic outcrops onto the black sand. The air smelled like rain. I suddenly remembered how isolated I was, how far I'd come on the bouncy speedboat from the city.

"Tell me."

"It's just that ... well, we have a thief in town," Vismar confessed. "He's been stealing from many of the hotels."

I shook my head, somewhat confused. "A thief's not all that bad," I said.

"You're right," Vismar continued, "but he's been causing lots of problems for people around here. They told him to stop, he wouldn't listen. So they hired someone to come from the city to take him out to sea and ..." He made a gun with his index finger and thumb and then clicked it in his mouth. Suddenly, I preferred the cocaine boats.

"Why would they do that?" I asked. "They could have just put him in jail."

"He'll just get out again and keep stealing," Colo interrupted. "All of us in this village are poor, we have nothing. He is the only one who steals. That's not fair."

"Makes sense." I said it but didn't mean it, or I hoped I didn't. "When is this happening?"

"Tonight, si Dios quiere," Vismar said. God willing. "It's very exciting for all of us. But you shouldn't even be thinking about it." All of this was to say that even the biggest problem in town shouldn't have concerned me, or any of the other beachgoers, and that I was safe.

———

I WAS FIVE YEARS OLD WHEN I STARTED TAKING PIANO lessons from a woman named Sandra Marlem Muñoz. The year I was born, she'd moved to New York from the Colombian city of Cali to pursue a career in music. Sandra was in her thirties when I first became her student. She used to come to my house on Tuesdays after school.

"*Hi*, Jordan! How are you?" she would always say in her singsong, accented English. Everything about Sandra was musical. Her heels clacked against the wooden floor; her metal bracelets jangled as she walked. If my dad was home they would speak Spanish, a language that I did not yet fully understand but that sounded like music itself. Hers was a flying staccato, typical of Colombia, my dad's a slow, more exaggerated Argentine Spanish that sounded almost like Italian.

During breaks, Sandra would play songs from her country. The small upright piano in the corner of our living room smiled as it came to life with pulsating, arpeggiated salsas and arabesques. A far cry from the slow drone of my attempts at Beethoven and Bach, her music was pure energy, and it was loud. "I want to learn those," I would say to Sandra as she and my mother drank tea after my younger brothers and I were finished with our lessons. "Please, Sandra, I want to play those."

I was a child then, and I did not know many things. I had no idea at the time that a long-running armed conflict had been shaking Colombia to its core—that when most Americans thought of the country in the upper-left corner of South America, they thought of cocaine, of Pablo Escobar and the narcos, and of communist guerrillas hidden away in the jungle. Colombia reminded them of targeted assassinations of soccer players, of air strikes and bombings, and of entire cities and villages paralyzed by war. They thought of the drug-running boats that I was so worried about in Ladrilleros.

But Sandra never spoke of these things when we were together; my window onto Colombia was Sandra's music. Besides soccer tournaments like the World Cup qualifiers and the Copa América—which, as a born-ready Argentina fan, I watched without fail—just about the only time I ever thought of the country was when I was with her. And all I can remember, now looking back, was sitting beside her at the piano each week and watching over the years as my slow scales transformed into the rambling melodies of the songs that I'd so desperately wanted to learn when I was just starting out.

After my first year in college, I was offered the opportunity to see Colombia for myself. It was a chance encounter through the Wildlife Conservation Society, the organization that runs the zoos and aquariums all over New York—these were the stomping grounds of my childhood, when I used to visit with my parents and younger brothers and stare wide-eyed through the Plexiglas at howler monkeys scratching their underbellies and hippopotamuses wallowing in the mud. WCS SUPPORTS WILDLIFE CONSERVATION AROUND THE WORLD, announced the signs at the zoo, though I never gave this fact much thought until I was older and actually decided to try to work for them. In school I'd become obsessed with the idea that the survival of those same species in the wild was deeply intertwined with the decisions and destinies of ordinary people, that perhaps my job could entail telling stories illuminating those relationships, in order to help encourage a greener path forward.

One day, the WCS office in Colombia called me back. If I wanted to spend a month helping with their communications efforts, based in their office in the city of Cali but traveling around the country, they would have me—the drug violence and guerrilla warfare had been waning for about two years already in the places where I'd be going, they told me, and there were rumors of a peace deal in the works that could end the conflict for good. The official travel policy of Princeton University, which funded my trip, was more cautious. I would have to sign my life away on several waivers, saying that if I died at the hands of drug traffickers or paramilitary militias, the university was free from liability; it soon became clear to me that everyone whom I told I was going to Colombia had similar fears, whether or not they expressed them aloud. This was far from reassuring.

My first thought was to call Sandra. I'd stopped piano lessons many years earlier, but our families remained close. "Oh my God!" she exclaimed. I could hear her smiling on the other end of the line. "You must go! You can stay with my grandmother in her house! She will take care of you!" Besides her grandmother, Sandra offered to introduce me to her cousins and friends, sprinkled throughout Cali, with whom I could play soccer under the lights and take road trips to nearby swimming holes and bustling Andean markets.

With that, suddenly, my outlook changed, aided not least by my own eager imagination. I envisioned a homestay with this sprightly grandmother, sharing a cup of sweet Colombian coffee on a porch shaded by mango trees as the sun came up; I imagined venturing off on my own, visiting rural outposts and wildernesses and documenting people's stories about how nature shaped their worlds. It would be like the movie *The Motorcycle Diaries*, I thought—like the story of a young Ernesto Guevara's transformative motorcycle journey through South America. He and a friend traveled from Argentina

to Colombia entirely by land and river: they visited leper colonies in
the Peruvian Amazon; spoke with disenfranchised copper miners in
the Chilean desert; slept beside breathtaking glacial lakes in the Patagonian highlands. His journals, upon which the film was based,
reflected a similarly deep sense of all of the many human and environmental injustices that characterized the places he'd passed along the
way. This was, of course, what would eventually radicalize Che Guevara the soldier, whose Marxist revolutions helped inspire the very
guerrilla forces that would terrorize Colombia for more than fifty
years. But Che the soldier was a very different man from Ernesto the
student, and it was Ernesto the student who was far more interesting
to me: the young man in his twenties who set off wide-eyed on an
anxious journey that would give him a new lens with which to view
the world.

It didn't hurt my imagination, either, that I come from a family
that has long traversed the different corners of this earth. Some of the
most memorable moments of my childhood were spent sitting beside
aunts and uncles and grandparents as they told me, in a spellbinding mix of English, Spanish, and Arabic, histories of a family that
seemed forever destined to be on the move. As with most travelers of
their time, they were driven by circumstances beyond their control—
religious persecution, economic opportunity, political strife—and
yet they hadn't failed to pass down tales of the new cultures and en-
lightening experiences that they'd encountered on the road. I'd long
been living vicariously through the stories of my grandfather, my father's father, himself a classmate of Guevara's in medical school, who
grew up in Buenos Aires and spent many years as a young doctor
backpacking and training in the Argentine countryside before even-

tually moving to New York. Abuelo told me of his father, my great-grandfather, a Syrian Jewish immigrant to Argentina at the turn of the twentieth century who worked as an itinerant salesman on horseback in the Andes Mountains; there, as the story goes, the Arab Jew from Damascus became Argentine, learning Spanish from folk songs and card games, sitting around bonfires with gauchos, and sleeping in ranch houses along his trade route. Many of his relatives and compatriots, also fleeing religious persecution in the old Ottoman Empire, found their way to other nations of Latin America—among them Mexico, Venezuela, and Colombia—where they built new lives and families and identities. On my mother's side there was the great-great-great-grandfather who led a caravan of one thousand camels along the famed Silk Road, trading carpets and textiles and spices in cities like Baghdad, Aleppo, Isfahan, and beyond; other Baghdadi Jewish ancestors made it as far as Shanghai and Mumbai. In the stories it sounded easy, their everyday bumps in the road smoothed over in favor of historical drama and tall tales. There seemed to be no port where their wanderings hadn't reached, and no place where there wasn't an adventure to be found.

I arrived in Cali on a Friday in August. No warnings did justice to how oppressively and impossibly hot it was in the city—the third largest in Colombia, known also to be the world capital of salsa dancing, and whose main water source was the Cauca River that flowed through the outlying shantytowns of corrugated-metal-roofed dwellings. Sandra's grandmother, Abuelita Ana, was ninety-six years old and bedridden, a kind woman who lived with an aide named Olga on the bottom floor of her two-story home. Each night Abuelita Ana would smile and ask me about my day, usually over a shared dinner of bland, creamy pasta that I ordered in because she forbade me from leaving the house alone after the sun went down. One night, when the two biggest soccer teams in Cali were playing each other, I listened longingly beside the front window as the city erupted in cheers with every goal. This was not because she was being cruel—precisely the opposite. She was trying to do the little that she could to make sure I was safe. The door would be locked after dinner, and she would take the key with her into her bedroom just after 7:00 p.m. On those warm nights, without reliable internet in the house or much of anything else to do, I took to writing detailed accounts of each day's events in a black marble notebook, not thinking I would ever write about my travels in earnest—I simply did it to pass the time.

I spent the month in and out of Sandra's grandmother's place, mostly working in the WCS Cali office to translate rather dull conservation news bulletins but sometimes arranging short excursions to rural field sites throughout the country. I came to crave these trips, quickly realizing that I preferred the slow pace of Colombia's countryside to its dusty, raucous cities, and in just a few weeks I covered a tremendous amount of geographical area without much direction—on a map, it looked like an unfortunate game of connect-the-dots. I spent time with villagers who were developing a turtle sanctuary along the river Sinú, in the wetlands of the northern Córdoba Department, where I went fishing with schoolchildren and picked fresh papayas for breakfast. I visited the magnificent Darién Gap on the Colombia-Panama border, one of the most dense, unforgiving rain forests left on earth—and witnessed hundreds of Africans, Asians, and Caribbean islanders attempting to cross it on foot in what was a desperate, near death march to reach the United States. And I traveled to the small town of Ladrilleros, on the country's rugged Pacific coast, where I met Colo and Vismar.

———

THE NIGHTS IN LADRILLEROS WERE LONG, AND LOUD. THE ferocious tapping of rain on the tin roof kept me awake for hours, and just when I thought I'd dozed off, the earth-ending roar of thunder rattled my little wooden shack and the thin mattress upon which I slept. In the room beside mine, a couple from Boyacá made loud noises throughout the night. When the rain finally stopped, the frogs began their symphony until dawn.

My favorite times in Ladrilleros were just before bed, when the couple from Boyacá had wandered off somewhere to look at the stars, and Vismar and Colo and I lay in the hammocks outside of the wooden shack for hours and compared our countries. Neither of them had ever been much farther than Ladrilleros or its closest city, Buenaventura, yet they dreamed of going to the United States. Vismar told me how he'd been saving for years to go to college in the United States, to become an engineer. He had two hundred dollars to his name so far, and he made it sound like he was close. Colo did not have such plans, though he asked me if I would mail him knockoff Nike sneakers when I got back to New York, saying that he would wire me the money.

"When are you coming back?" they asked me, more out of curiosity than anything else. I guess they expected me to say something like "a few months" or "next year." I was asked this by many Colombians, most of whom lived in places so remote that it was a miracle I'd made it there in the first place.

"You know, I'm not sure, it's very hard to take a trip like this," I said, dodging the question.

"Ah." They nodded but did not seem to understand, for a few days later: "Hey, when did you say you were coming back again?"

"I don't know."

One older Colombian woman, who happened to sit beside me on a wooden boat tour through the mangroves of Ladrilleros, told me that if I ever came back to Colombia, I should not return to the Pacific coast. No, she said: Instead I should visit all the many places in her country that she'd heard were beautiful but where she herself had never been. The white-sand beaches of Tayrona National Park, beside the Caribbean Sea; the rainbow-colored waters of Caño Cristales; the Amazon jungles of the South.

"Oh, and how could I forget the Magdalena River!" the old woman added. "The greatest river in Colombia."

The Magdalena River. It wasn't in the tourist guidebook like the other places she mentioned, but I recognized its name immediately, for so many people in Colombia spoke of it to me with an almost-religious fervor. "A place you must not miss," they said. It seemed to be every Colombian's dream to someday travel the 950 miles of its course, though not many people had actually done it. The Wildlife Conservation Society had a project in a community somewhere along its banks, but it was in the Magdalena Medio, the Mid-Magdalena, where at the time they had told me it was still too dangerous to go.

I landed back in the States a few weeks later, at that point more curious than fulfilled from my trip, and without having laid eyes on the great Magdalena River. But I did not forget about my time in Colombia. In college, friends studied things like economics and history and biology, while I devoured everything to do with Latin America, reading books like *One Hundred Years of Solitude* and *The Old Patagonian Express* and dreaming of a second chance to travel there. The next summer I spent on a grant in Argentina and Bolivia, tracing the route of my great-grandfather—the long-ago traveling salesman in the Andes—and seeing for myself that ours was indeed a family forever on the move, linking one place with the next, exchanging goods and stories and cultures as they wandered. I realized the value of a journey with a singular thread, one that could connect seemingly disparate places and people. And I was beginning to figure out that telling these stories was what I wanted to do with my life.

The Magdalena was waiting for me when it came time to decide on a topic for my senior thesis. I'd decided I wanted to spend time with people along a river, and I was surprised that it took me so long to find my way back to my old journals from Colombia, written in the sweaty heat under Sandra's grandmother's careful curfew in Cali. Immediately I was reminded of the glimmer in people's eyes when they told me of their country's greatest river; indeed, in Colombia there is no river that is more important and revered than the Río Grande de la Magdalena, which flows through just about every kind of landscape—mountains, jungles, plains, and swamplands—before emptying into the Caribbean Sea. The river is central to the history of Colombia and much of South America, serving as the setting for several of the continent's most famous novels (by Gabriel García Márquez), the birthplace of some of its most popular music (from regional genres like cumbia and vallenato, which arose from the valleys, to global superstar Shakira, who was born in Barranquilla at the river's mouth), and the source of myths and legends that have since touched lands far beyond the river's banks. In Colombia's heartland, the Magdalena is a major source of life. The old woman in Ladrilleros had said to me, "To understand the river is to understand the country."

Maybe I wanted to understand Colombia because it is always changing, always coming up with something new. By late 2016, just a few months after my first trip, a landmark peace deal had been signed, and the worst of the guerrilla armies were supposedly demobilizing. Areas of the country that were previously off-limits were now ostensibly back on the map, and there was renewed hope after more than fifty years of conflict. But every few months there were regressions, too: in the absence of the guerrillas there came political upheaval, threats of a return to arms, killings of environmentalists and local activists and ex-combatants, and the strengthening of dissident criminal groups, all stoking fears of a relapse into violence. And all the while, through the ups and downs of hope and despair, there were stories of ordinary people doing what they could to help, often in the most extraordinary of ways.

One thing was for certain: the Colombia I met in 2016 was a far cry from the Colombia I came to love just two years later, when I did indeed return, though at the old woman's advice I did not go back to Vismar and Colo in Ladrilleros or to anywhere else I'd been before. I returned to Colombia with the goal of traveling the entire length of its most important river, from source to sea, south to north, over the course of four weeks. With school in the way, this was all the time that I had; an ambitious goal, but by no means an unattainable one.

Figuring out how I would do it was another question entirely. The Magdalena River of the storybooks was a river of life, revered for its romantic journeys through landscapes with astounding biodiversity. I soon came to dream of long voyages by steamboat through the dense, misty wilderness, of siestas spent cruising by in a hammock, without worry, lulled by the hum of the ship and the buzzing of the jungle. A life lived by river seemed impeccable in its simplicity—you never had to worry about where you were going.

Indeed, such adventures, which I very much wished I could have myself, were impossible now. The Magdalena of the storybooks was the Magdalena of the past—before the violence and ecological collapse—and the river that's left now, plundered and pillaged, is a shadow of what it once was. Passenger boats no longer ply much of its course; instead, using any means of transportation I could, from pickup trucks and buses to mules and wooden canoes, I would have to make my way through villages and towns alongside the river that has long dictated their fates. But this was not an insignificant thing. Before and after my trip, I spent many months poring over a musty two-volume set called *Crónica grande del Río de la Magdalena*, perhaps the single most diverse and comprehensive collection of Magdalena writings ever published (the books were heavy and long out of print; for a while I had them on long-distance loan from a library in upstate New York—every three weeks I would return the copies and immediately request them back again, for I was clearly the only one after them in years). I studied the river's course, its ecology, and the names of its port towns incessantly, all of which were repeated over and over again in its hundreds of traveling tales across the centuries. But the Magdalena, like most major rivers, has a long history of being described mainly by those travelers afforded the perspective of floating on it and looking out. This to me did not seem too different from peering out the window of a train, always soothing but unable to offer a fuller picture of a place in time before it recedes into the oblivion of the past. What about the people who lived beside the river, I thought, in places where the steamboats did not stop?

I remember, in one such case, coming across a description of a fishing settlement along the river as observed by a Swiss professor, Ernst Röthlisberger, from the deck of a steamboat in the late nineteenth century. Of the farmers and fishermen he spotted along the shore, he wrote, "When they need salt, lead for their nets, and guns or knives, they fill their canoes with bananas or dried fish and navigate downstream to the nearest village; there, they sell their goods, buy what they need, and then sink back into their nothingness.

"These people live in indolence," Röthlisberger continued, "without religion, and without manners, not subject to any authority and are yet happy in their ways."

This seemed, like so much else when it came to Colombia, to be a misunderstanding. Steamboat travelers hardly had to pay much attention to the fishermen in shacks and the villagers in towns and hamlets that have long lined this artery of a nation, this express highway that once connected the country's beating heart to its shimmering sea. It was easier and more common to exoticize, as Röthlisberger did—to brush them off as "bestial" or "wretched" or otherwise banished to their own seclusion. In making my way by land rather than only by water, I would be spending time getting to know the people of the Magdalena, not just the epic river itself.

This book will take you along with me, on a journey down one of the greatest rivers in South America that you may not have heard of. No longer is a book on Colombia guaranteed to be all about

Pablo Escobar and his narco henchmen or all about the seemingly never-ending violence that has dragged the reputation of an entire country and its people through the mud. This one surely isn't. I will always remember the reckoning I had on a sweltering May afternoon in New Jersey, toward the end of my third year in college; I lay on a dusty-blue couch with the dorm room windows wide open, the fan blowing in my face, and three books on the coffee table that told me, all at once, not to travel to the Magdalena River—that it was an unforgiving place, a lonely place, a place where nobody should go anymore. And then, just a few days later, near the river's upper reaches, I was watching Atlético Huila defeat Patriotas Boyacá in penalty kicks in the quarterfinals of the Colombian league championship and belly laughing at the chaotic pitch invasion that followed; weeks later, I was playing with children in the warm waters of a Magdalena tributary; then eating kibbe and hummus, familiar Middle Eastern comfort food, just miles from where the great river finally meets the sea.

Nor does travel writing have to rely only on fleeting, one-time encounters anymore. In a globalized world of shared languages and cultures in common, there exists every reason to start a conversation—and with WhatsApp and Facebook, several of my own conversations that began on the road have continued online, easily, for many years after a first and only meeting, our impressions of each other deepening and acquiring layers over time. To that end, this book is as much a journey down a river as it is an immersion into the lives of the ordinary people who find themselves alongside it. This book will share stories of the everyday challenges and joys faced by Colombians in their homes and communities—like Vismar and Colo and the thief of Ladrilleros—as the country tries to move on from a devastating conflict and the people of the heartland begin to pick up the pieces. It is a journey filled with stories of the very real struggles of humans and nature, but it is also a journey filled with stories of strength, marked by passionate people who have long remained devoted to living meaningful, deliberate lives in the midst of hardship and solitude and don't plan on stopping now. It is a story about finding beauty in places where travelers sometimes least expect it.

To understand the river, they told me, is to understand the country. But Colombia is perhaps the most misunderstood country on earth.

PART ONE

Alto Magdalena

Upper Magdalena

In Colombia extremes of climate, of altitude, and of civilization meet. There the present and the past live for a moment side by side, almost on terms of equality; before both give place to the waiting wonder which is the future.

BLAIR NILES
Colombia: Land of Miracles
1924

I

The Legend of
Doña Juana

JUANA WASN'T MEANT TO RUN AWAY FROM HOME. AT least, that's how the legend goes.

She was from a wealthy Indigenous family that is thought to have lived, thousands of years ago, in what is today the southwest corner of Colombia. Her parents were endowed with an immense quantity of gold—that mythical gold of El Dorado that, thousands of years later, the Spanish never found. (The Indigenous people knew where the gold was all along, according to their descendants. Just look at their tombs, which were adorned with the stuff. The Spanish simply didn't know where to look.) Not everyone had gold, though—not even close—and because they possessed such a tremendous quantity of gems and jewels, Juana's family enjoyed a lifestyle that was lavish compared to that of the rest of their village.

But Juana was a rebellious child, spoiled by the wealth of her family. As she grew older, she fell in love with a man whom her parents did not accept. And then, one day, after her parents gave her a particularly harsh scolding, Juana decided to run away for good and take her family's riches along with her.

For days she followed river gorges and slick, muddy trails deep into the highlands. Through the thick air and torrential rains, she trudged on, eventually reaching such an altitude where the dense rain forests gave way to the rolling landscape of the Andean páramo, with its volcanoes, low-lying shrubs, and frigid lagoons.

To this day, these lagoons are where the major rivers of Colombia are sourced, and none is more revered than that of the Magdalena, considered for as long as anyone can remember to be the most important river of them all. At its surface the lagoon seems placid, set in a depression among thick grasses and surrounded by a number of small hills, yet it is rumored to be many miles deep. It was in the Laguna del Magdalena where Juana is said to have met her untimely end.

How exactly she disappeared is an often-debated topic of conversation among farmers living in the gateway villages to the páramo. I have heard people, most often the elderly, fervently discussing the tale of Doña Juana—the woman who ran off with her family's gold—among the colorful open-air produce markets of the Colombian highlands, where unrefined panela cane sugar is sold in the form of bricks and live chickens are pulled from mesh bags and wire cages. Everyone seemed to have their own version of the story—and in between customers, everyone seemed to have time to tell it. Sitting on a chair beside her bags of grain piled up on the floor, an older saleswoman wearing a red sweater and dark-blue checkered apron told me that

Doña Juana was cursed by her parents and was swallowed by the lagoon in its earliest act of magic. Every now and then, a nearby panela salesman would chime in, purporting that, in fact, it was said that along the banks of the lagoon she encountered bandits who roamed the farthest reaches of the mountains. They tried to rob Doña Juana of her gold, and instead of allowing them to do so, she threw herself and her jewels into the headwaters of the Magdalena.

But in every version of the story, Doña Juana drowned—consumed by the lagoon along with her treasure—and from that moment on, the Laguna became enchanted and forever hostile to visitors.

"Our elders always said to approach the Laguna with respect, to go quietly and to not cause too much commotion," a young man named Arturo told me. He claimed to have been to the Magdalena's source two or three times in his life. "They told us, 'If you want to go to the Laguna, you mustn't make too much noise, because the Laguna is a difficult place, and in an instant, it can cause all sorts of trouble.' Once, a group of six of us tried to prove that this was a lie—we started yelling and laughing, and suddenly we couldn't escape its grasp. We couldn't escape because waterspouts started pouring down from the sky, right into the center of the Laguna, and wintry clouds came in from all sides and trapped us. We struggled to get back to the trail."

Almost sixty years ago, a woman named María worked with her sister to cook food for men maintaining the trail to the Laguna, and now she recalled the many times she laid eyes on it: "You could've been passing through on the sunniest, warmest of days, but when you least expected it, the wind picked up and a storm came in." Another woman declared that the only way to calm the Laguna's fury was to throw a live rooster or guinea pig into its waters.

I was told that to this day the site remains "sensitive" and must be approached with great caution—if there is too much noise, a violent wind picks up, and the Laguna de Doña Juana, as it is also known, shrouds itself in thick clouds, as if it were angry. Visibility decreases to the point of disorientation, and the soft ground around the edges is prone to sinking. Several people have drowned in recent years, a reminder of what happens when you get too close.

———

THE LAGUNA BECAME ENCHANTED AND FOREVER HOSTILE TO VISI-*tors.* For centuries, people have been talking about the Magdalena— not just the Laguna, but the entire river—as "enchanted." A vital source of water and life for so many generations of communities comprising a vast majority of Colombia's population, the Magdalena often flows right through people's towns. It enters their homes as fish on the table, their schools as the history of their country, their streets as maritime cargo and passengers that fill their trucks and carts. The river passes by men resting on its banks, in the shade of guadua trees, taking a brief respite from the oppressive heat of the lowlands be- fore returning to work in its waters; by women washing clothes in the muddy shallows; by the millions of cows grazing in flooded pastures. It makes sense, then, that such a vast discharge of life has often been understood through legends and folktales.

These stories began with Indigenous peoples, who built enor- mous stone statues that interpreted the lives of the lizards and the monkeys and revered the natural gods that gave all of them life. When the Spanish conquistadors made inroads into the continent in the sixteenth and seventeenth centuries, often literally carried on the backs of the subjugated natives who already knew the terrain so well, they were so astounded by the immense biodiversity of the tropical Americas that they believed it to be the site of the Garden of Eden and the creation of the world—and the Magdalena, once a jungle river rushing through deep green landscapes yet untouched by the destructive hand of humans, was believed to have been one of the four rivers of paradise from the book of Genesis. Though scientists like Alexander von Humboldt—the Prussian botanist who led several famed expeditions into Colombia at the beginning of the nineteenth century—later dispelled these notions, by no means did spiritual and religious associations with the river ever entirely disappear, even as its pristine natural backdrop did.

Most common today are the oral histories, myths, and legends—like those of the Laguna—that run the length of the river basin and vary from town to town. They remain in the local lore and serve as warnings or teachings about the river for those whose lives depend on it—the Laguna de Doña Juana, for example, served for years as a cautionary tale for the many traders who passed it by while crossing the mountains. Other stories of the Magdalena have reached far beyond the places where they began: "I know every village and every tree on that river," claimed Gabriel García Márquez, Colombia's most famous and beloved writer, in a 1989 interview with the newsmagazine *Semana*. In his books, which have been translated into hundreds of languages and read all around the world, García Márquez so vividly portrays the intersection of the magic and the real along the Magdalena's banks that some villagers told me they believed his novels to reflect the true stories of their lives.

There are the remaining megalithic statues, animal-like figures carved into four-meter slabs of volcanic rock, which still preside over the gorges and rolling hills of the upper reaches of the river, studied by archaeologists attempting to solve the mysteries of a civilization that thrived and then disappeared without a trace. Children who have nothing to play with but scraps of river flotsam, which they manage to fashion into shimmering toys to pass the time. Change makers, regular villagers and townspeople, helping in the most unconventional of ways to pull their communities out of the violence that destroyed livelihoods for so many years. Artisans and engineers who have dedicated themselves to their trades with such steadfast devotion that for them, despite the turbulence of the world swirling all around, time seems to stand still. Each of these encounters takes place in such a vastly different setting that it could at times feel like an entirely different country altogether, if it weren't for the unmistakable Magdalena threaded throughout the varying landscapes, carrying sediments from places past.

————

THE LEGEND OF DOÑA JUANA AND THE ENCHANTED Laguna is almost prophetic, reflecting the last one hundred years of the history of not only the Magdalena River but all of Colombia. Years ago, during the "golden age" of the 1920s, '30s, and '40s, triple-decker steamboats so stunning they could have been a thing of fairy tales shuttled passengers and cargo along the Río Grande de la Magdalena from inland cities to the coast and beyond. Equally luxurious railroads followed the course of the river of gold, which flowed through thick rain forest and harbored vast quantities of fish and wildlife. Common sights and sounds included howler monkeys screeching in the trees and caimans sunning their leathery backs on the shores. The Magdalena River was the crown jewel of Colombia.

Toward the latter half of the twentieth century, though, the situation worsened. Prospectors of all kinds stripped the forest of its trees and shot the caimans for sport. Unrestrained by the roots of the jungle, land spilled into the river and built up upon itself, creating embankments of sediment that blocked the passage of the steamboats in many critical places. What remained of the navigable river was shrouded in decades of war, under constant threat from armed groups vying for control of the land, and the Magdalena quickly became an epicenter of the Colombian armed conflict, which began in 1964 and has left more than 260,000 people dead and several million displaced over the course of nearly sixty years. There were days when fishermen would see more corpses than boats floating down the river and when townspeople would witness assassinations from their doorsteps.

The ever-shifting fortunes of the Colombian people have long mirrored the rise and fall of their country's greatest river. Perhaps this can be attributed to the sheer numbers: 80 percent of Colombians live within the Magdalena River basin. Thirty-eight million of the country's 49 million people depend on its waters in one way or another. The river's banks touch eleven of Colombia's thirty-two distinct departments: Huila—where the Magdalena is born—then Tolima, Cundinamarca, Caldas, Boyacá, Antioquia, Santander, Cesar, Bolívar, Magdalena, and Atlántico, where it finally reaches the sea. The people of the Magdalena River valley live in communities as large as major cities with hundreds of thousands of inhabitants (Neiva, Barrancabermeja, Barranquilla) and as small as two or three fishing huts on patches of riverside land. In between the extremes are towns and villages of varying sizes, whose inhabitants have jobs mostly related to the river and its surrounding land, in industries such as fishing, canoe transport, agriculture, and cattle ranching. There are a few who are able to eke out a living by promoting the river's conservation—from leading community-based conservation and cultural preservation projects to working in local- and department-level government environmental offices—but not nearly enough. Apart from some notable exceptions, the financial situation is often dire, and in some cases, people do not have work at all, turning to more informal sources of income or subsistence fishing and farming in order to feed their families.

Many of the people who live along the banks of the Magdalena are also often among Colombia's most vulnerable communities. Refugees from Venezuela fleeing a catastrophic situation in their home country continue to settle wherever they have family ties, unloading at dawn with their few possessions from the dark cover of idling cattle trucks draped with black tarps. Afro-Colombians, the descendants of enslaved people brought over from sub-Saharan Africa, live closer to the Caribbean coast in lands known for being the origin of the rousing rhythms and undulating accordion melodies of vallenato and cumbia music. And people of Indigenous origin populate the highlands of the Macizo Colombiano—the Colombian Massif—a geographical clustering of the birthplaces of the most important mountain ranges and rivers of Colombia that once allowed for the natural convergence of tribes from surrounding regions who used the river gorges as networks for trade and cultural diffusion.

After the first one hundred of its 950 total miles, the river ceases to tumble over smooth, gray boulders and exits the craggy massif, setting its course almost precisely due north, and quickly widening as it descends into the muggy lowland plains that have come to be known as the Magdalena River valley. For much of its course, the Magdalena flows through these lands—tierras calientes, steaming-hot valleys once draped with megadiverse jungles and unhindered savannas. Just before reaching the coast, the mountains on either side of the valley dissipate, and the river loses itself in a vast seven-thousand-square-mile mess of low-lying marshes and wetlands. It then regains its shape for its final hundred-mile run toward the Caribbean Sea.

Follow the Magdalena far enough upstream, however, and you get a very different picture. A narrow, raging torrent of water at this altitude, the river first leads you past the farms and pastures in the rolling hills, then upward through still-forested mountains via rain-slicked trails, and finally, higher yet into the treeless páramo landscape that is unique to the high South American tropics. This is where, at nearly eleven thousand feet above sea level, Doña Juana was supposedly swallowed by the Laguna. The only way to reach the Magdalena's source is a two-day journey on horseback from the closest official settlement along its banks: a village of approximately ninety families called Quinchana.

2

Rumors of the Magdalena

TO GET TO QUINCHANA, I WOKE UP AT HALF PAST FOUR IN the morning to the sound of roosters crowing in the dark.

I was staying in a wooden guesthouse in San Agustín, the nearby municipal seat just downstream, where the midday sun brought comfortably warm temperatures but night arrived with the howling of dogs and a silent chill that descended upon the Colombian Massif like a cold blanket. The roosters broke the stillness well before sunrise.

I took a motorcycle taxi to the center of town—near the Agricultural Bank, where the only daily shared pickup truck leaves for Quinchana at six—and stood on the corner with a woman in a pink sweater and a man in a gray button-down shirt. I was expecting one other person to join me: Luis Manuel Salamanca, an anthropologist nationally renowned for his work on the UNESCO World Heritage Site in San Agustín—the collection of enormous megalithic statues

built before the eighth century c.e. that put the town on the map—
and other sites in the massif. At quarter to six he was still nowhere to
be found. I gave him a call.

"Come to my house!" he said excitedly. "Come! I'm five blocks
away." Staying on the phone, I followed his directions and hurried
down the silent, foggy street, breathing hard from the altitude and
my growing anxiety, until I heard the echo of his real-life voice calling my name. I turned to see his short, hunched figure through the
morning mist, waving me over to his house on a grassy plot of land
along a cobbled side road leading away from town. Clearly, he was
running late, but he made it seem like everything was perfectly under control. In his house, which was adorned with ornaments of
Christ, he calmly drank hot chocolate milk out of a plastic yellow
mug. He gave me a cup with a soggy, doughy bizcocho breakfast pas-
try mixed in.

"We have four minutes," I said, glancing nervously at the clock.
Luis was quiet. He finished his chocolate, calmly gathered his things,
and then motioned for me to walk out the door as if I were the one
holding him back all along. When we got to the Agricultural Bank
on the corner, the woman in the pink sweater and the man in the gray
button-down shirt were gone.

We're sunk, I thought. *We'll just have to wait until tomorrow.*

Still, Luis said nothing. He looked around for a few seconds,
then suddenly started walking back on the road toward his house. I
followed him, and sure enough, within a few minutes, a white pickup
truck with a black solid covering over its bed rumbled through the
intersection ahead of us. These camionetas are a common way to
get around in Colombia, often serving rural roads where buses are

hard to come by. The lucky first few passengers claimed seats in the air-conditioned interior cab, while the rest were relegated to benches facing each other along the edges of the covered bed, hopping on and off through the truck's open-ended rear. Luis whistled the camioneta down, and we hurried to climb on.

In our case, both the cab and the bed of the truck were completely full—not to mention the roof, which was crammed with straw bags of vegetables and concrete building materials—so we would have to stand on the flat tailgate, holding on to the cold metal roof rack as the truck made the bumpy ninety-minute journey along just fifteen miles of winding back roads to Quinchana. But at least we were on board. Passengers, ranging from older women draped in wool to young schoolchildren dressed in the green-and-white uniforms of Huila, hopped on and off in small hamlets between San Agustín and Quinchana. Most of the hamlets had just a handful of houses along the road, some doubling as small general stores that sold refrigerated beverages, nonperishable foods, and rechargeable cell phone minutes. The woman in the pink sweater from the corner got off at Villa Fatima, the most impressive of the intermediary hamlets, which had a playground and a small plaza. The homes we passed along the way were all very rudimentary in construction, with terra-cotta, metal, or thatched roofs, and sat close by this single-lane paved road that grazed the wall of damp, mossy rock along tortuous, narrow ledges.

———

MY HEART WAS RACING. INITIALLY, IT HADN'T EVEN crossed my mind to set foot in Quinchana. Colombians I'd met from other parts of the country had warned me: "You shouldn't go any farther into the mountains than San Agustín," they said. "It gets complicated." That's because, from 1993 until 2016, just two years earlier, Quinchana was a "red zone," meaning it was a no-go area that was infested by guerrillas. The Revolutionary Armed Forces of Colombia (FARC)—the largest rebel group of guerrilla soldiers in the country, with a reputation scary enough to deter even the bravest of travelers—controlled the surrounding mountains, including the area around the Laguna del Magdalena, and came down periodically into towns to resolve disputes and to discipline those who did not abide by their rules.

You could always tell the difference between a Colombian military man and a guerrilla soldier, I was told, by their shoes: the military wore black leather boots with laces, while the guerrillas wore rubber galoshes fit for long stays in the muddy, buzzing jungle. My biggest fear, echoed by almost every foreigner who has written about travels in Colombia in recent years, was that I would be kidnapped by the FARC and taken into the wilderness, held for every ounce of ransom they could squeeze out of me. That I was American, I'd heard, made me a potentially valuable target for them—guerrillas knew there were no lengths to which my government wouldn't go to bring me home (or so I'd hoped). And I was just twenty-one at the time, but that didn't mean my poking about the embers of a conflict couldn't get complicated. A graduate student at Princeton, where I was to be a senior in the fall, was going on his second year of imprisonment in Iran, his history research declared an act of espionage against the government. What, I thought, might the wrong person make of me and all my questions? After all, I remembered from my first trip, that was how you got in trouble in Colombia—by asking too many questions about the wrong things.

It had almost happened to the late British writer Michael Jacobs, who encountered the guerrillas while passing through Quinchana on a trek to the Magdalena's source around 2010—a dangerous time to be in any part of Colombia, let alone this pocket of remote countryside—and portrayed the town through a lens of utter fear. "It was a landscape of ghosts and tragic memories, of killings and kidnappings, of farms taken over by the FARC," he wrote in his book *The Robber of Memories*, "of children robbed from their homes, of army searches and reprisals, of inhabitants who had learnt to survive by not telling anyone anything."

The FARC has always thrived in places where the quiet, remote hills offered protection and seclusion. The group was formed more than fifty years ago in a rural farming settlement just like Quinchana, among an isolated patch of mountains farther north in the central Andes. "La Violencia," a vicious civil war fought in the countryside between liberals and conservatives, claimed more than two hundred thousand lives between 1948 and 1958. By the early 1960s, a group of communist peasant families, invigorated by the travails of their earlier fight, established an enclave in the hamlet of Marquetalia.

Fearing a communist revolt similar to that of the Cuban Revolution just five years earlier, in 1964 the Colombian military invaded Marquetalia and attacked the farmers, and out of the militia that resisted, the FARC was born. Over the years, other FARC-inspired groups rose up, like the National Liberation Army (ELN), an equally terrifying guerrilla group that would spring up shortly thereafter in the Mid-Magdalena valley, becoming the second largest of its kind in the country.

The FARC dominated many Colombian villages and towns for nearly half a century—but now, on paper at least, there seemed little left for an outsider to be afraid of in the way of the guerrillas. The more populated areas of the country, including the entire Magdalena River basin, had been rid of the FARC several years earlier, and the final nail in the coffin should have been a peace deal signed with the government in 2016. But the rumors about rural Quinchana, and the thought of being sequestered in a jungle camp somewhere in the cloud forest, had still been enough to deter me. That is, until I reached San Agustín, where Luis Manuel Salamanca assured me with all of the conviction he could muster that Quinchana's darkest days were now behind it. He admitted that the region, like much of the country, was still plagued by a complex web of armed groups— among them drug traffickers, right-wing paramilitaries, and dissident guerrillas—wrestling for control of the resource-rich land and lucrative smuggling corridors that the FARC had left behind. But as far as we were concerned, Luis said, Quinchana was nothing more than a peaceful farming village set among tall green hills, perforated only by the steady sound of the Magdalena rushing below.

———

AS THE SUN ROSE, THE COLOMBIAN MASSIF BEGAN TO stir. The fog lifted: In a clearing along the pavement, a woman milked a bloated cow. Red-and-white buses filled with schoolchildren fought

for passage on the narrow roads with horse-drawn carts and cargo
mules. At every turn, as our pickup truck swerved around countless
bends with steep cliffs, it became increasingly apparent just how far
this vast landscape seemed to extend. There were no jagged peaks
or high sierras in sight, though I knew we were heading in that
direction—for now, just a fertile, rolling knot of river gorges and
dome-shaped hills sitting at a temperate six thousand feet above sea
level. Brown and white cows skirted around small clusters of tall,
slender trees to reach the very tops of the hills in search of good grazing. Small farmhouses, only specks drowned out by an undulating sea
of green, seemed to be virtually unreachable, located where no road
could ever possibly lead and a mule trail would have to suffice. All
the while, the coffee-colored Magdalena was visible more than two
hundred meters below, rushing through a green gorge fed by waterfalls and clear creeks tumbling down from every direction. At some
points up ahead of us, the clouds appeared to touch the tranquil land,
creating the illusion of steam rising from the farms or even from the
river itself.

Everything in Colombia seemed to be under construction. In
much of the country, double-lane highways were the next big phase
of development, such that irresponsible truck drivers would no longer have to attempt palpitation-inducing passes in the face of oncoming traffic, and on almost every major thoroughfare I saw men at
work building them. Here, tucked away in the Andean South, rain-
saturated pavements often buckled into a mess of roots and wet dirt,
closing the main roads for repairs and forcing us onto back routes
that were uncomfortably high in the hills. The nearly two-hour ride
to Quinchana hardly seemed to faze Luis, who at sixty-four years old

rode beside me on the outside of the truck for the better part of the trip, tightly gripping the roof rack in silent defense against the powerful jolts caused by every bump in the road. He was spry for his age, accustomed to long walks to reach field sites in the countryside. His most prized possession was his slender silver bicycle, which he used to get around town and spoke of with a great deal of admiration, in the same way a cowboy admires his horse.

Luis had a gentle face, round with a ball-shaped nose, and trimmed, curly gray hair. His smile offered a sense of security and warmth akin to that of a fuzzy sweater. Yet he was a discreet man who did not speak much, and when he did, it was in quick, quiet bursts that were difficult to understand. Eventually, as we neared Quinchana and some other passengers disembarked, he reluctantly took a bench seat after the insistence of the rest of us on the outside.

———

WE ARRIVED AT SEVEN THIRTY IN THE MORNING AT THE start of the small town strip of Quinchana, in front of a home that also served as a general store. The owner was a thirty-year-old woman named Karen Mayori Salamanca. When I asked, she and Luis Manuel Salamanca said they were not related, which was not all that surprising—in the Colombian countryside, especially in smaller towns with large families deeply rooted in generations of history, last names have inevitably begun to repeat themselves.

We were here in search of an archaeological site called La Gaitana, filled with some of the prehistoric granite-slab statues that made the massif famous. Most exciting were the extraordinary megaliths of nearby San Agustín, of course, which presided over the spectacular UNESCO World Heritage park of trimmed lawns and gravel trails, almost like a zoo of stones. But La Gaitana, Luis said, would be like seeing statues in the wild; it was hidden away on a mountainside and surrounded by years of overgrowth from the times when Quinchana was off-limits. The farmers and archaeologists who watched over it during those days did so at their own risk, because it harbored part of their own collective past.

I knew this about Luis's plan for the day in Quinchana, but not much more. "Better to go before it rains," he repeated to himself, looking up toward the thick gray clouds above our heads that had burrowed themselves in the crevices of the valley. "Better to go before it rains."

The cool morning air smelled pleasantly of burning firewood. Outside Karen's place, two toddlers were running along the small grassy curb between the doorstep and the street. One was Karen's twenty-two-month-old daughter, Dana—who wore green, dirt-caked sweatpants and a ragged white shirt that barely covered her round toddler belly—and the other was her twenty-month-old nephew, who wore a red tank top, shorts, and black Nike sneakers. The two children were play companions, minded by a large, menacing turkey with a drooping red wattle and a lengthy snood.

I initially found it strange that the village of Quinchana is technically called Puerto Quinchana (Port of Quinchana), since it is not a seafaring port but one of the remotest mountain towns in Colombia, hundreds of miles from any ocean. It had only one main road, a dusty mix of dirt and stones that ended with the town itself. The whole day, I counted only a handful of motorcycles, plus the scheduled camioneta that brought us there and the truck that would bring us back to San Agustín later that afternoon. The road was lined by about a dozen small buildings along the approximately quarter-mile stretch that constituted the main town limits. The buildings were mainly homes, which, like Karen's, also doubled as small stores.

Later that day, Luis and I would walk to where the road ended, at the edge of the calm Quinchana River just before its perpendicular intersection with the fast-flowing Magdalena. The Río Quinchana was nothing more than a shallow creek on a bed of stones during the dry season, and on the other side of it was a muddy mule trail that proceeded to climb a steep hill parallel to the Magdalena before disappearing over a ledge. This long, winding trail, if followed for two days straight on horseback, would eventually lead to the Magdalena's source.

Luis said he'd passed through here for the first time almost fifty years earlier, with his father, in August of 1968. They were visiting family in western Colombia, past the high-altitude Laguna del Magdalena and back down a mountain pass leading to a town called Valencia, in the Cauca Department, on the other side. This route helped to build Quinchana over the course of the twentieth century, he told me, connecting the town with the western edge of Colombia and the road to Ecuador. Long before a road wide enough for cars reached Quinchana, traders arrived from San Agustín and elsewhere on the backs of mules and horses to access the trailhead to the pass, moving all sorts of merchandise across the pass to the other side of the country. Salt, corn, and panela were among the things they carried, raw goods sourced straight from the lands of the massif. From the other direction, mostly from places like Ipiales near the border with Ecuador, came processed materials like clothes, shoes, and leather. For centuries, almost anything transported between Huila and Cauca, historically two of the most productive and important departments of Colombia, had to pass through this mountain port town, earning it the official name of Puerto Quinchana.

The worst of the guerrilla years all but put an end to the vibrant trade that once graced the trail to the Laguna, though, and to the presence of outsiders in "Puerto" Quinchana in general. "Even foreigners used to come," Karen told me as we sat by the entrance to her home. "But the guerrilla period put an end to that."

Aliria Salamanca Semanate, the owner of another convenience store in town and also of no relation to Luis Manuel Salamanca, recalled a conflict on a neighbor's farm years ago that the guerrilla forces had to "resolve," which meant that she and her family had to sleep somewhere else for three days. In 2004, she said, the guerrillas forbade villagers from voting in local elections, "ruling like an army."

Instead of traders passing through Quinchana with salt and panela, drug traffickers began to monopolize the path to the Laguna, hoping to move their merchandise under the cover of the wilderness and by paying "taxes" to the FARC in exchange for safe passage through their territory. In a place like Quinchana, you are constantly reminded of your isolation. Reaching neighbors' homes, especially in the higher hamlets, takes several hours. There was hardly a police presence in the main town area, and a serious injury on a mule trail could very well lead to death, with the closest medical clinic nearly two hours away in San Agustín. So harvesting and trafficking illicit crops became a more or less unchecked way to make money, and in Quinchana, opium was the crop of choice. Here, the opium boom began in the early 1990s, lasting for approximately ten years, and families who wouldn't otherwise do so turned to it as a possible solution for unforeseen expenses such as unpaid medical bills. Farmers who didn't want to grow opium themselves hired out their land to others, and they, too, made payments to the FARC in exchange for protection. This was the case throughout much of the massif, but more than anywhere else in the farthest reaches of the Upper Magdalena. Here, guerrillas and drug traffickers took advantage of the very same riverbed "highways" that were first used by the pre-Hispanic Indigenous groups who once inhabited the land.

In Quinchana, people said, the drug trade fostered an atmosphere of pervasive violence. "People from these very villages started to cause problems," Karen Mayori Salamanca told me. "Sundays are market days here, and you couldn't even go out at all because there would be one or two dead each week." Husbands were slaughtered, often drawn reluctantly or unwittingly into the heart of the trade, leaving widowed wives and a generation of children searching for answers about their disappeared parents. Long after the opium trade declined and the guerrillas retreated even farther into the wilderness, an eerie silence remained cast over Quinchana—no longer was it a thriving port in the mountains but a sleepy farming village like the dozens of others around it. No longer was the mule trail to the Laguna a centerpiece of the regional economy but a poorly maintained hiking path.

———

KAREN'S HOUSE WAS WHITE AND MADE OF WOOD, THE paint flaking off the exterior walls. Beside the brown door hung a piece of plain letter paper reading, SE VENDE POLLO—"chicken sold here"—in tall, oddly spaced black handwriting that looked like that of a child. Inside, there were three rooms, one for each function of the building. The main room was the store, dark and musty, and it had no windows. A set of plastic tables and chairs sat next to the entrance. The glass cabinets in the middle of the floor were packed with a chaotic assortment of seemingly random provisions. Teddy bears and coloring books rested next to hygiene products and lighters, while school supplies shared a shelf with rubbing alcohol, wrapping paper, and canned lentils. Beans, oil, eggs, and mangos rounded out the list. Two smaller rooms lay off to the side of the main room. The kitchen was small, but with enough space to fit a refrigerator, gas stove, wooden sink, and cutting table, as well as an open-air window, through which the family deposited their food waste into a buzzing mess of vegetation and dirt, where a small population of chickens clucked about. The third room was the bedroom, containing two low full-size beds with old, depressed mattresses and a small analog television set. It was in this room that Karen, her husband, and their two children slept.

When we arrived in the morning, she served us a hot breakfast consisting of a healthy portion of eggs scrambled in butter with diced tomatoes and scallions, along with two small arepas—flat, round patties of grilled maize—and a cup of syrupy hot chocolate. Later in the day, we would go on to spend several hours sitting in Karen's store, which was frequented by local quinchaneces looking to buy either food or other supplies of some sort. But first, Luis said, it was time to take advantage of the morning weather for our hike to La Gaitana.

At still only about eight thirty in the morning, the weather was chilly but humid. We set out from Karen's place along the road, turning off by a two-story green-and-white building alive with the morning chatter of schoolchildren, and descended on a dirt path toward the riverbank.

We passed a barren soccer field before reaching a rickety wooden suspension bridge that crossed high above the narrow Magdalena, from one green ledge to another. Though it didn't seem significant, the bridge was one of the few in all of Colombia that directly connected two of the country's three cordilleras, or major mountain ranges, all of them branches of the Andes. The Western, Central, and Eastern Cordilleras fan out in a northbound direction from the mountainous cluster that is the massif, eventually spreading so far apart that one can only be seen from another on the clearest of days. Crossing the footbridge, however, we were able to walk from the Eastern Cordillera (Quinchana) to the Central (La Gaitana) in a matter of seconds, since the width of the river valley here could be measured in feet instead of miles.

PASA SOLO UN ANIMAL, read a sign that hung over the entrance to the bridge, warning people that it could only support one animal at a time. Behind us, a horse stepped on the bridge while Luis and I were still crossing, and with each stride the horse took, the bridge swayed. We hurried off. Between the gaps in the old wooden planks, the dark Magdalena was visible below us, flowing over boulders and stones, its brown water turned white by the rapids. At this point, it was still a wild mountain river hardly touched by a human hand. I took a deep breath of the cool air, knowing that along the Magdalena it wouldn't last for long. Even here in the massif, Luis told me, they were planning something: a network of dams that would flood the farthest reaches of the Upper Magdalena valley, nearly as far as Quinchana, sparking fears of immense environmental and archaeological losses in the region. Luis, a passionate conservationist, was involved in the efforts to stop it.

The hike that lay ahead would be only about a mile long—that much I'd gathered from Luis while we were still at Karen's. But I didn't realize how strenuous that mile would be until we reached the other side of the bridge and were faced with a scramble up a steep, muddy hill. Luis wore black galoshes, having anticipated the messy trails. I had no such understanding of the terrain; my flimsy sneakers quickly became soaked with groundwater and mud. Eventually, the horse and its caretaker from the bridge caught up to us as we rested halfway up the hill. The horse carefully plotted each step of its path, zigzagging slowly up the hill at a strong, steady pace, even while carrying a heavy load of those straw bags filled with vegetables and cement. The man wore a bright yellow Colombia national soccer team jersey and played loud, thumping reggaeton music from a cell phone in his pants pocket. The sound was muffled, but I could make out the high-pitched voice of the Puerto Rican singer Luis Fonsi, of "Despacito" fame. I noticed everywhere I went in Colombia that smartphones seemed to be more prevalent than in 2016, even in the most rural and impoverished parts of the country like Quinchana, where reliable service still did not reach.

We exchanged pleasantries. "Are you Don Dubier's son?" Luis asked him, using a title of respect as a formality ("Don" for men and "Doña" for women).

Dubier . . . Luis had not mentioned we would be meeting someone.

"No, sir, I am Don Victor's son," the man replied politely, scratching his head. For someone who had just hiked halfway up such a steep incline without stopping, he stood with remarkably good posture and did not seem to have to catch his breath. I was bent over beside him.

"Ah, okay." Luis thought for a moment. "Do you know where Don Dubier lives?"

"Oh, yes." The man, waiting for the question out of respect so as not to assume our business, knew exactly where Don Dubier lived. "Don Dubier lives up there." He pointed high up the hill to the roof of a tiny house peeking out over a ledge, hardly visible to the naked eye. I took out my binoculars to make sure I'd heard him right. Indeed, it was a colorful place that appeared to be teetering on the edge of the cliff, obscured by farmland and overgrowth on all sides.

We walked with the man and his horse along the trail for quite a while. I once again took note of Luis's alacrity despite his age—this time, it was because he stopped at every opportunity to pick up a bottle cap for a donation campaign for children with cancer. Sometimes he would spot a plastic bottle somewhere off the trail, go to great lengths to reach it, remove its cap, and then leave the bottle in the thick vegetation.

After a while, the trail became less steep, and though we were still palpably moving uphill, it was clear we had reached the first small ledge on our way up the mountain and were walking along it. Above us were some steep grassy pastures leading to another ledge, flatter yet, where a school was visible, marked by its green and white paint. We'd be there soon enough. To our left was an expansive vista that overlooked the Quinchana town center in the foothills. Smoke was rising from invisible farmhouses higher in the green mountains above town. Upriver from the bridge we'd just crossed, the Magdalena carved its way toward taller, forested hills shrouded in clouds.

At one of the lookout points, there seemed to be a new monument of sorts under construction. So far, only the stone pedestal had been built, flanked by two flat wooden benches.

"It's going to be a religious icon to protect the trail," the man announced as we passed it by. Then, very nonchalantly: "This part of the path causes people problems at night. You'll be walking in the pitch black, and you'll just sense that someone is following you."

I could hardly imagine walking alone on this path now, let alone in the dead of night, with the farthest lightbulb at least half a mile up or down the mountain. "What do you mean?" I asked, looking over my own shoulder for no reason at all.

"No one's there," the man told me. "But the animals sense it too. I was riding my horse once, and when we passed by this area the horse just took off running, running like it was possessed. There was nothing around, of course, but it didn't matter. The horse sensed something."

That something, I would later learn, was thought to be a mythical creature known as El Duende, a goblin-like spirit that is said to roam the shores of the Magdalena River, looking for people and animals to possess. Later, a skinny ten-year-old boy named Jhon Alexander would sit on a tree stump for nearly forty-five minutes and tell me everything he knew about El Duende, which was mostly what his mother and father had told him: that the Duende snatches children playing down by the river's edge, shepherding them into tunnels covered by the brush before killing them in the darkness of the underworld. Once, while he was playing with his friend Omar, he heard the creature for himself—it sounded like an infant crying, he said, and the two boys took off running. They were terrifying stories, yet Jhon Alexander did not seem afraid, speaking with all of the poise and gravitas of a grandfather telling the story of his life. The backdrop of misty mountains dwarfed his small figure, and tiny beads of sweat trickled down his dark cheeks, which were flushed red, for he had just returned from playing in the fields.

Though most often told to children as a cautionary tale for good behavior, it was striking to see how many adults still embraced and recounted reported sightings of El Duende as they would any regular event. "Some people say that they see it, and that it looks almost like a child," Karen told me in her store. "Others only hear sounds: sometimes the sound of crying, sometimes singing, sometimes playing, things like that."

The ledge where we stood with the man and his horse was known in town as La Chorrera del Duende, or Duende Falls, because it overlooks a narrow stretch of river rapids the creature is rumored to frequent. Karen was as straight-faced as Jhon Alexander and the man with the horse in telling such stories.

We parted ways with the man and his strong horse soon after La Chorrera del Duende, as Luis directed us off the trail and through some thick vegetation uphill to the second ledge, to see the La Gaitana School. Every turn seemed arbitrary to me, but Luis very clearly knew exactly where we were going. It was a long, one-room schoolhouse for children five to eleven years old. There was only one teacher. The two dozen students, concentrating intently on their lesson workbooks, became wide-eyed with curiosity when we entered, greeting us in unison: "Buenos días!" Clearly, they were in the middle of a lesson that we had interrupted. Luis and I apologized to the teacher, a young but tired-looking man who asked us to return a bit later when the children were having their recess.

A few feet from the school was the archaeological site we had come to find, my first glimpse of the famous megalithic statues of the Indigenous peoples of the Colombian Massif. Here at La Gaitana, the statues were relatively flat, upright four-foot stone slabs carved clearly with anthropomorphic images—they resembled monkeys with wide faces, round ears, and mouths bearing tall rows of teeth. Of course, the real monkeys were hardly around anymore, driven away long ago to places deeper in the mountains where forests still stood; the same went for the tapirs, the spectacled Andean bears, and the big cats.

Still within view of the elementary school, dozens of small stone slabs on the ground marked a bumpy clearing of small grassy mounds. "An ancient cemetery for children," Luis said quietly. The gravestones were just dark boulders, overgrown with moss and sometimes stacked upon one another. Some of the bodies had been excavated over the years for a number of reasons, Luis said, while others remained hidden and fully decomposed below the surface. I wondered how many outsiders in the past fifty years had been privy to what Luis had brought me to see—how many would have made the two-hour journey to Quinchana, along the winding roads, and then the mule hike along muddy paths, all under the threat of guerrillas, to find the remnants of a people that no one knew much of anything about. I thought about what might have caused this civilization of artisans and long-distance traders to vanish so many centuries ago. An all-encompassing war, perhaps, or some sort of inescapable disease—then again, these were the secrets tightly guarded by the silent mountains of the massif, the rumors of the Magdalena. We could only guess.

We wandered around the area for a few minutes, Luis moving nimbly between the sites despite the difficult terrain of tall, wet grasses and thorny shrubs that brought me great trouble. I took note of the different types of rudimentary fences that delineated property, including lines of barbed wire connecting upright wooden posts, and a special kind of gate that could be unlocked by carefully removing several cross-sectional logs from their corresponding holes. As Luis and I were hardly deterred by such obstructions and moved freely about people's private land, I decided that these devices existed mainly for the purpose of keeping out wandering animals as opposed to humans. Finally, after peeking into several smaller farming huts to ask for directions—happening upon gatherings of cooking women who spoke in hushed voices around glowing fires—we found ourselves close to the top of the hill, outside of an extravagantly colored home enveloped by the brass-infused melodies of a salsa playing over the speaker system. The famous Don Dubier, whose full name was Dubier Males and who served as the president of the community council of La Gaitana, had perhaps the nicest view of all, overlooking the town of Quinchana and the mountains behind it. Below us, the trail that had brought us most of the way was a winding brown line that crisscrossed the hill down to the riverbank.

Dubier appeared a young man, and his home was essentially an extension of the mountain, with two terraced floors and a slanted tin roof parallel to its slope. An eccentric, open-air patio was adorned with dark-red leather couches and two dining tables surrounded by colorful plants. Behind his house was a small fish farm with green water and several large machines for grinding the hard stalks of sugarcane that grew on his property. The mangled cane scraps from the previous day's work lay in a massive heap beside the mill. Above that, farther uphill, were his crops: mainly sugarcane, but also coffee and yucca. He offered us "café tinto," a kind of coffee typical to the Colombian countryside in which the grounds are mixed with fresh panela (unrefined cane sugar) and water and boiled on a smoky, wood-burning stove. The sweet drink is served hot in small, round cups—not unlike Turkish or Arabic coffee—and consumed at all hours of the day. I sipped on mine while listening to Dubier and Luis, who'd met each other at a computer-skills class back in San Agustín, fervently discussing national politics and Quinchana's newfound peace.

"Quinchana has a new face," Dubier said, referring to the end of the guerrilla era and the coming of peace in the town, as we sat overlooking the spectacular gorge that lay below us. From up here, farms plastered the lower foothills of the mountains like a quilt of a dozen shades of green, with smoke rising from individual patches toward the low-lying clouds. In the 1980s, before the start of the opium years and the arrival of the guerrillas, Quinchana saw a healthy number of visitors as an offshoot from the more accessible San Agustín. Now, people are once again touting the town's renewed tourism potential, especially as the trailhead for the Laguna del Magdalena. Walking with Luis along the town strip later in the afternoon, we even ran into several Europeans loading up a gray mule and some horses with a local guide, preparing for a trek into the páramo.

"What I tell my students now about the peace process is that it's like buying an abandoned farm," Luis added. "You have to put a lot of money and a lot of work into it, and then wait for a while, hoping for the results to show."

———

IT WAS NEARLY A YEAR AFTER I MET HIM THAT I FOUND out that Luis Manuel Salamanca had been murdered. I was sitting in a college classroom with dark-wood walls and heavy antique doors of the kind that are supposed to make you feel far more important than you actually are, until you hear about something like this. I found out from a Facebook post by a mutual friend of ours in San Agustín. He'd uploaded a gray-scale photo of Luis in front of a microscope, hunched over his desk just enough that you could still make out his round nose and gentle eyes.

They'd killed him in cold blood. Luis was leaving for one of his regular nighttime walks, which took him through his neighborhood of quiet, grassy lanes down to the Parque San Martín and back home. But he didn't make it even a few steps from his house before someone shot him twice, from behind, the bullets piercing him once in the back and once in the head. I imagined Luis's beloved silver bicycle still waiting beside the door. "It's just been devastating" was all his friend could muster. "Don't forget that every day in Colombia another social leader is killed."

Indeed, it's become an all-too-common pattern in rural, post-FARC Colombia: social leaders and local activists of all kinds are targeted in systematic killings by a complex web of armed groups who deem them threats to their interests, often within regional power vacuums created by the demobilization of the guerrillas. Luis's family said that he'd "gotten into problems with someone," and though I only knew him for a handful of days I found it hard to believe that Luis Manuel Salamanca could have problems with anybody at all. But despite his quiet demeanor, the anthropologist was an outspoken defender of land and water and cultural heritage in Colombia; his activism is thought to have been at the root of his assassination. Indeed, the definition of "social leader" is broad, and the carnage has been equally wide-ranging: conservationists have been slaughtered for opposing environmentally destructive enterprises like mining and logging; scientists and teachers killed for promoting education and peace; Indigenous leaders murdered for protesting land grabs and human-rights violations. As its defenders are eliminated, Colombia's countryside—home to immense reserves of biodiversity found nowhere else on earth and to forests that serve as a vital carbon sink for our warming planet—continues to suffer at the hands of ever-encroaching miners, traffickers, and ranchers. A conservative government seemingly indifferent to their cause has meant that most of these crimes against social leaders go unsolved.

In the days and weeks following Luis's murder, it was difficult to parse through the details from a distance; between pangs of grief and fear of retribution, hardly anyone close to him wanted to speculate, especially to an outsider like me, on the exact motivations behind the attack. I was reminded that as a traveler in a complex country, there was still very much I would never know. But the story of the anthropologist's assassination in San Agustín, of the killing of "the Most Illustrious of the Agustinianos," was all over the national news; on social media there was an outpouring of admiration for his contributions to a deeper scientific and cultural understanding of Colombia's past and his fight to preserve it. In the days following his murder, hundreds took to the town streets, candles in hand, for a march demanding justice. A reward of 10 million pesos (almost three thousand U.S. dollars) was offered for any tips that might lead police closer to his killers, but besides that, any official investigation that existed quickly fizzled. Still today, nobody is quite sure who did it.

———

THE SEVENTY DEGREES OF THE AFTERNOON FELT WARM enough to induce a siesta-like spell back in Quinchana, where people were retreating to their homes for several hours' rest when we returned. Earlier in the morning, Karen had asked Luis and me what we wanted to eat for lunch—when we requested chicken, she peered out her window and replied with a grin, "Which one?"

The chicken was fresh and tender, grilled over a charcoal fire and served with a plate of rice and lentils and a bowl of mealy corn soup. After lunch, we spent the better part of an hour trying to locate the oldest person in Quinchana, a ninety-eight-year-old man named Don Juan, who lived near the trailhead at the end of town and could apparently recount the town's history with total lucidity. According to several of the villagers, Juan was an enigma: half-deaf, with several missing fingers, yet still able to take care of himself alone in his house. When we found his house, we were surprised to see gray smoke billowing out of the cracks in the door and the slats in the old wood that held the building together. "He cooks with a wood-burning stove," a neighbor told us. Perhaps we'd failed to yell loudly enough. "No, he must have gone out for more wood," the neighbor suggested. "He will be back soon."

But we spent three more hours in town without seeing any sign of him besides the thick smoke that continued to pour out of his home. "A ninety-eight-year-old man can't move that fast, and the town only has one road," I said to Luis, hoping he knew something I didn't.

"Another spirit," Luis replied with a slight grin, and that was the end of the conversation.

And then, as quickly as the early-morning camioneta almost passed us by in San Agustín, a gray Ford pickup truck came racing down the quiet road well before we were scheduled to leave. With one shrill whistle, the ever-alert Luis brought it to a screeching halt. We had happened upon an archaeological maintenance vehicle that was shuttling a group of Luis's colleagues between routine site checks, and thanks to Luis Manuel Salamanca, the most illustrious of the agustinianos, we were able to hitch an unexpected ride out of Quinchana, a place I was never meant to visit in the first place. We sat, tired and dirty, in the uncovered bed of the pickup truck as it bounced and snaked its way out of town. And that's when it began to rain.

3

The Mohán

IF DOÑA JUANA'S BAG OF GOLD ENCHANTS THE MAGDA-
lena River at its source, it is the Mohán who guards the riches of its
waters as it begins to flow through the heartland. Perhaps the most
important mythical creature of the Upper Magdalena—the entire
first third of the river, from the Laguna to a stretch of impassable
rapids near the town of Honda—the Mohán has humanlike features,
with long, straight hair and a body permanently scorched by the sun.
His vices are distinctive: he is a heavy drinker of Colombian aguar-
diente, a strong sugarcane liquor, and is often seen smoking a thick
cigar to ward off the clouds of swarming mosquitoes that descend
upon the river at dusk. He is said to inhabit the deepest and most
treacherous eddies of the Magdalena, surfacing from his underwater
caverns to terrorize local fishermen. When the Mohán appears, ac-

cording to many people who said they have felt his presence, an ominous black shadow envelops the river, and a shrill whistling sound pierces the air. "I felt goose bumps all over," one boatman, named Alfonso, remembered of his hair-raising encounter with the Mohán while fishing with his cousin. Like Jhon Alexander with El Duende, "we went home as fast as we could." Twelve years on, the experience still haunted him.

The Mohán is often blamed for accidents concerning the river. If someone drowns in the turbulent waters—and especially in cases of women disappearing while washing clothes in the river (for he is known for pursuing and abducting women in all sorts of situations)—it is said that the Mohán is exacting his revenge on the human population. Some along the Magdalena believe that's because the Mohán protects against the overexploitation of the river's resources. Within the Upper Magdalena, the Mohán legend is most prominent in the Tolima Department, just downstream from where the Magdalena tumbles out of the hilly massif into the sticky, humid lowlands. In these parts, the river is far from a narrow torrent of rushing water—it flows smoothly through relatively flat land, often splitting into several branches that form a web of water passageways meandering around islands of tangerine and mango trees in an ecosystem that has historically teemed with fish and wildlife. But the lands along the Upper Magdalena—as with much of the rest of the river, too—have been mismanaged and pillaged. Forests have been cut and burned, dams planned and constructed, fish caught well past their limits. Indeed, the Mohán is now often blamed for poor catches of fish. "The Mohán makes sure the fishermen don't catch anything," said another boatman, whose family has for generations shuttled passengers up and down the Upper Magdalena. "The fishing net would feel heavy in the water, you'd feel it moving around, and then you'd take it out and it would be empty. That's the Mohán at work."

4

River of Gold

"SALCHI!" FELIPE ORTIZ YELLED TOWARD A DECREPIT-looking structure perched atop a stone wall overlooking the river.

"Pasa!" a voice replied, telling us to come up. We climbed the steep staircase and arrived at a grimy, open-air repair shop filled with spare boat parts, life jackets, and piles of miscellaneous items that seemed to have accumulated there over several decades. Clunky metal fans groaned in the background, no match for the oppressive heat of the tierras calientes and the large black flies that came along with it. A foul smell, which rose from the muddy banks of the river, wafted through the shop.

Felipe, a heavyset man and a smoker, was sweating profusely. I felt bad for him: when his niece, a classmate of mine, told him that I would be spending a few days in his hometown of Girardot, I don't believe this was quite what he'd expected. Girardot is one of Colombia's hottest cities, a cursed honor, and most visitors come for its water parks. They do not stay for long, retreating after a day or two back to the cool air and palliative drizzle of Bogotá, just a three-hour bus ride into the highlands. That we were instead here by the river, suffering from the flies and the odor and the heat of the day, was no one's fault but my own. I came to Girardot looking for its gloomy market, reeking of colorless, twitching fish and puddles littered with scales; for its mostly abandoned wharf, now considered the "bad side" of town; and for the Río Magdalena, once the town's main attraction, which no one came to visit anymore.

Felipe and his family were warm and generous hosts. They graciously offered me a room in their house, owned by Felipe's mother, seventy-eight-year-old Doña Teresa. It was quintessentially Colombian in its layout: Single-level, with open-air corridors laden with Catholic ornaments and framed family pictures. A courtyard beside the kitchen let in the afternoon rains, which lightened the heavy midday air. We rested in hammocks stretched out in the main room of the house, around a lunch table and television set, and beside a counter piled high with flats of warm, brown eggs. Doña Teresa, a lively and religious woman, crossed the street morning and evening to pray the rosary and go to Mass, accompanied always by her bashful live-in housekeeper, Amparito.

The night I arrived in town, Felipe and I had dinner at American Burger, a packed Girardot fast-food joint, where diner-style red-white-and-blue menus were written in Spanish and old-fashioned doo-wop rock songs were mixed in with brass-band salsas. We wore restaurant-provided latex gloves while we feasted on several dozen fried chicken wings doused in sweet barbecue sauce, sweating through our shirts because, although we paid the two extra dollars to sit in a room with air-conditioning, the air-conditioning was broken.

This was my introduction to Girardot. I expressed my hesitations to Felipe the morning after I arrived, when he offered to take me to all of the harshly uninteresting places I was hoping to go.

"Don't worry," Felipe said while we were driving to the wharf, through crowded streets lined with street-cart salesmen touting fresh guanabana and pineapple juices, and past slaughterhouses filled with moaning cows and bleating goats. "La Negra Lady will protect you." He said this very matter-of-factly, as though I were to understand.

The Black Lady? Surely I'd misheard him. "Who is La Negra Lady?"

He unzipped his small handbag and pulled out a black revolver. "La Negra Lady." He grinned.

The handbag was strapped tightly to Felipe's body as we made our way up to the repair shop above the wharf. Felipe quickly found a fan to call his own and positioned himself on an overturned paint bucket in the corner. Alejandro Rodríguez, known among friends as Salchi, sat filling out paperwork at a small table by the top of the stairs. He wore a light-blue collared T-shirt with the logo of his company, called La Barca del Capitán Rozo (Captain Rozo's Boat), emblazoned on the breast pocket. I wondered who Captain Rozo was.

"I bet that Felipe had to tell you, 'Watch out, because this area is *dangerous*,'" Salchi said to me. He had very wide eyes.

"Yes," I said. Also, a policeman wielding an assault rifle had glared intensely at us when we parked the car. That helped give it away.

Salchi leaned back in his chair and sighed, rubbing his forehead. "That's the stigma we have here in Girardot, you see?"

Felipe interjected. He'd been examining a shotgun that was on the floor beside him and snapped it into place. "Well, wait, it's just that I don't—"

"Felipe, relax, I'm just using you as an example." Salchi turned back to me, and Felipe turned back to the shotgun, holding the scope up to his eye and pretending to aim toward the river. "But Felipe is from Girardot, and if you weren't coming to the wharf, he wouldn't otherwise come here on his own. You get what I'm saying?"

I understood. So long as Girardot's own residents wouldn't set foot in the river zone, neither would visitors.

"When Girardot turned its back on its port," Salchi said, "it became a forgotten place." That's when the wharf was abandoned, he continued, and became a gathering place frequented only by thieves and squatters. Since those days—the 1970s, more than forty years ago—the neighborhood has taken strides toward bettering itself. The wide, steep stone steps leading down to the water's edge were cleaned up; La Barca del Capitán Rozo built a new, colorful floating restaurant with yellow chairs and blue tablecloths for riverside lunches. It had two motorized launches for quick rides on the river. As with any town, Salchi said, Girardot had its faults, but here was an example of an area that was slowly turning itself around from what he called a "sunset" on its glory days.

And in the years before Girardot's decline, things were glittering—in this town and along the entire length of the Magdalena. The very man who was the company's namesake—the late Captain Rozo, a Girardot native whose full name was Rafael Rozo Vega—was, I later learned, one of the most important and venerated boat captains in the history of the river, somewhat of a legend in the lore of the

Magdalena, though he himself commanded a rather short route. He began working on Magdalena riverboats when he was just ten years old, becoming a full pilot at sixteen. In 1939 he established his service to ferry passengers between Girardot and the stretch of impassable rapids farther north, where they had to disembark and travel several dozen miles by land before reaching any port with a direct steamboat bound for the sea. These steamboats (and, before the steamboats, rowboats most often powered by subjugated people of Indigenous and African descent) were how the Magdalena earned its distinction as a natural highway—a "fluvial artery," as most Colombians put it— that connected the coast with the nation's heart: the fertile lands of its interior, and the cool, temperate climate of its capital, Bogotá.

When put that way, it sounds like a relatively straightforward journey. But Bogotá, a landlocked city set on a plateau in the eastern Andes, is nearly fifty miles from the closest Magdalena riverbank as the crow flies. The tortuous climb through the hills makes the distance feel much longer. Captain Rozo lived in an era before sufficient roads were built snaking through the rising jungle to allow automobiles to easily reach the Bogotá plateau, and before a ninety-minute plane ride allowed most travelers to admire the entirety of the Magdalena's sinuous curves and milky-brown waters from above. The most common way to reach the capital from the river was an arduous journey on muleback, most often beginning at the Honda rapids and ascending almost nonstop on an old Muisca native trail until reaching the high Andean plateau. There was considerable excitement, then, when a direct railroad connection opened up between Bogotá and Girardot, just south of Honda—and Captain Rozo was the crucial link in the chain that made it accessible. Without him, passengers would be left with no other option but the mules, stranded at Honda or beyond.

The bridge that once carried the railroad across the river could be seen from Salchi's office atop the wharf. Now a sparsely used pedestrian walkway, it was thin and gray, built from dreary steel trusses that were rusting from age and little upkeep. Just upriver, a newer, bright-yellow bridge carried a much busier roadway across the Magdalena, a sign of the fate that had befallen the town.

"We were a village that became a city," Salchi said of Girardot, "and now we've become a village once more." All of the development that had come with the prosperity of the Magdalena—expansive, smog-filled streets, a metropolitan population of more than one hundred thousand people—was just an illusion of great magnitude, a village still dressed in a city's clothing. Now, asked Salchi, what was it all for?

Girardot rose to especially great heights because of its strategic location along the Magdalena, but it also tells the boom-and-bust story of plenty of other places, from cities to towns of varying sizes, that once enjoyed the same prestige of simply being located on the banks of Colombia's greatest river. Towns that now hardly carry much weight on a map of the country—places like Honda, Ambalema, Mompox—are renowned in the collective memory of the Magdalena, emboldened and starred on the first European atlases of the Spanish colonies and referred to consistently in the dozens of more recent travelogues and stories written by locals and foreigners alike.

The town names mostly remained the same over the years, but there were, of course, vast differences in context. An eighteenth- or nineteenth-century traveler would emphasize the strength of the African and Indigenous bogas—referring to the rowers, initially enslaved and conscripted by the Spanish, who propelled dugout vessels called champanes along the Magdalena for hundreds of years. Transport along the Magdalena was long dependent on these bogas, who were subjected to insufferable, often fatal working conditions and widespread discrimination in society. Drawings portrayed them in overtly racist, animalistic tones, depicting their dark, bulging arms and synchronized chants as they thrashed their oars, dripping with sweat, struggling against the current. "Their tumultuous cries, peppered with curses, would be lost in the bowels of the jungles that lined the shores and the sleepy currents of the Magdalena," observed the nineteenth-century Colombian writer Manuel María Madiedo in his essay "El Boga del Magdalena." Many died on the job.

But by the twentieth century, the bogas were not much more than a wretched backdrop to the mammoth steamboats that cruised smoothly along the center of the river's tract. Before the steamboats, river travelers—even those as distinguished as Simón Bolívar, "El Libertador," who helped lead the independence wars against Spanish colonial rule and served as the president of Gran Colombia, the first independent nation-state—marked each day's end by setting up humble camp in small jungle clearings and on muddy embankments. Now, passengers could spend nights on the river itself, sleeping under mosquito nets in the cabins or hammocks of the steamboats. "In the journey the river performs a miracle, and time stands still," wrote Blair Niles, an intrepid American travel writer of the 1920s who traversed the river from Girardot to Barranquilla by steamboat in the days when the jungle was still buzzing and alligators were visible on every shore. "What was tomorrow? Or yesterday?" she pondered. "There could only be the Magdalena, sharing with us the flowing eternity of its dawns, of its dazzling noons, of its glorified sunsets, and the stormy brilliance of its nights."

These years, the 1920s, '30s, and '40s, were the "golden age" of the Magdalena River, when more than one hundred vessels regularly plied its course. It was when Rafael Rozo became Captain Rozo and began to ferry passengers between the railway station in Girardot and the steamboats to the coast. It was also when, being the most practical way to navigate through the country's rugged interior, the Magdalena gained the reputation of being the crown jewel of Colombia.

Salchi, Felipe, and I finished our conversation and decided to take one of the boats for a brief ride upriver. It was close to noontime, and the heat was so thick you felt as though you could reach out and grab it with your hands. But the sky was overcast, and the sun was hidden. For Girardot, a place where the heat of the equatorial sun can at times be too strong to bear, it was a perfect day for boating.

The company's floating restaurant was empty, and the two boats bobbed quietly off to the side. While Captain Rozo would have boasted larger vessels, these were nothing more than slender launches, with benches to fit only a handful of people each. We climbed into one while Salchi worked to ignite the motor. After a few yanks of the chain, it coughed and sputtered to life.

Salchi did not say much as we pulled away from the dock. Felipe pulled out an e-cigarette and inhaled—a long, deep breath. He used the thing relentlessly: "I'm trying to quit smoking," he told me earlier, as he proceeded to hotbox his pickup truck with the vapor's fruity smell.

A light drizzle began to fall, sprinkling our faces as we proceeded upriver against the swiftly moving current. The banks were brown and muddy, like the river itself. There were few signs of development at the river's immediate edge—mostly just greenery and trees littered by heaps of trash and torn plastic bags. Behind the trees, on the Girardot side of the river, you could make out a few lean-tos and shantytowns, and along the shore, solitary men were fishing. One threw a large round net into the river from a rocky outcrop on the shore. Another fed a single hook and line into the water from a long, slender wooden canoe.

———

THE WOODEN CANOE HAS LONG BEEN THE HEART AND soul of the Magdalena. Around since well before the days of the Spanish and the bogas, it remains the transport mode of choice for fishermen equipped with strings and nets, and for riparian communities that were largely ignored by the rise and fall of the steamboats. Now, many are fitted with motors, Yamaha or Suzuki, but there are still some that are slipped into the rivers each dawn, like arrows in the water darting silently but for the occasional splash and ripple of an oar. Our river excursion in Girardot wasn't to last longer than midday, but had we continued upriver long enough, in a few hours we would have reached the city of Neiva, the capital of the Huila Department and the Upper Magdalena, where an elderly man named Delfín Borrero has been hand-making these canoes in splendid colors for generations.

I met Delfín on a much brighter day on the Magdalena, when the clouds had parted, and sunlight pierced the shade of Neiva's riverside wharf. His work space sat next to a dirt slope that led down through the brush to the water's edge. There was no building with a roof, or any structure at all to complement the small area he called his own. Only colorful canoes—each painted a pair of bright colors, green and yellow, red and blue—perched on stands among a line of twisting trees. A little girl in a bright pink dress played joyfully in each boat, jumping from one to another, while her grandfather sat beside his creations, admiring his work.

"For forty years I've been doing this," said Delfín. He was a small man of seventy, thin and unassuming, but seemingly delighted that I'd come asking after him. He wore red pants and a yellow collared shirt that was faded by the sun. His hands were swollen at the joints and dry like sandpaper, the effect of his many decades of hammering and crafting wood. The location of his workshop hasn't changed much over the course of those decades, either—it was set in the same spot along the rustic, dusty wharf, just past a forty-foot-tall statue of the Mohán, the guardian spirit of this part of the Magdalena. Delfín was born into a family of poor fishermen, and when he couldn't afford a canoe to get on the river, he thought to try and build his own—despite the fact that he didn't know how and didn't have any equipment.

"I bought the planks and I went about building it little by little, with no real tools, just an ax and a machete," he said. He had few teeth and spoke quickly, excitedly. "It was extremely ugly, basically a box—it kept flipping me over in the water." He chuckled.

"Then a man came along, and he told me, 'I'll buy it from you.' I sold it to him for less than ten dollars, next to nothing. With that I bought a workbench, made another canoe, and got better at it from there."

The customers kept coming. At some point, Delfín realized he could make more money from building canoes than from fishing in them. Now, he's the preeminent boat maker in the area, selling them for some $250 apiece.

"I've made more than two thousand canoes of all sizes," he said of his forty years at work, pointing me to a new one he finished and sold last week. It was colored bright green, with a red border, but its planks were already scratched and the paint was peeling in the heat. "For me, it's an art. I'm an artisan here."

Though he works alone, as odds go it wouldn't be the worst bet to guess that any wooden canoe in use within the limits of the navigable Upper Magdalena, from Neiva to Girardot, had been built by Delfín. Across the riverbank, to the west of Neiva, the river splits off into several branches and forms a network of channels meandering around various fertile settlements known as vegas that are so thickly covered in greens that you can barely make out what the people's houses look like, or that people live there at all. "The people live off their land," a canoe ferryman named Alfonso told me. "Tangerine, orange, guayaba, mango—they live off of their own harvests," he continued. And in order to get to "mainland" Neiva, they have to ride in one of Delfín's canoes.

Delfín's workshop also functions as something of a shipyard, where Neiva's fishermen grab their canoes to put in the river. It's also where they return to sell their catch: beside the canoes on the wharf was a small fish market, protected from the rains by black tarps tied to the trees. I watched as one young boy turned over a bucket filled with heaving black creatures that looked like terrifying fish-frog hybrids, leaving them to dry out on the dirt floor.

Delfín smiled as he proudly walked me through the half dozen canoes that were on display—to me, quite the uneducated canoe observer, they looked identical but for their paint jobs, yet he went to great lengths to point out the intricacies of each: the angles at which the port and starboard sides sloped, the spaces between the seats. More than anything, I got the sense that I was the first person in a while to take a general interest in his work. "These three came out beautiful," he said, placing his hand on a boat painted bright green and yellow. His granddaughter didn't seem to notice us, climbing in and out of the splintery wooden creations that served as her private playground without a second thought.

"Do you like the canoes?" I asked the little girl. She nodded. "Are you going to build canoes when you grow up?"

She could not answer before her grandfather interjected. "She's going to study," he said, his smile giving way to an expression that was serious and stern. Suddenly he didn't seem as proud of his canoes anymore.

———

BACK IN GIRARDOT, THE HEADWINDS HAD PICKED UP, and small whitecaps began forming on the Magdalena. The drizzle was stronger now, stinging our faces as we continued upriver, powering our way against the current. Salchi turned off the engine for a few seconds to show me the strength of the river, and we started drifting backward almost as quickly as the motor had been able to propel us forward. A loud, ominous hiss accompanied us as we were carried back downstream—something like the sound of fine sand sliding down a metal tray.

"That sound," I asked Salchi, "is that the river?"

"Sand," Salchi answered. "Sand and sediment."

I looked around. We were precisely in the middle of the river, the shores far away. Felipe seemed equally puzzled. "No, what's the *sound?*" he tried to clarify to Salchi, pointing frantically to his ear as if he were speaking another language.

"That's what I'm saying. It's the sand being carried by the river."

"You're kidding." I was impressed.

"You haven't heard the saying around here?" Salchi was surprised. "*Cuando el río suena, es porque piedras lleva.*" When the river sings, it's for the rocks it brings.

The term "rocks" is generous: most of the audible sediments carried by the Magdalena are, individually, each smaller than a grain of sand. Yet over the course of millions of years, the Magdalena has been the principal contributor of sediments, sands, and seeds for the lands along its entire route, including the famous white sands of Cartagena's beaches and the islands along much of Colombia's northern Caribbean coastline.

The very sand the Magdalena carries also tells the story of the river's own demise. For more than half of the twentieth century, the forested jungles on either riverbank were eliminated without restraint. The land was cleared and flattened in order for lumbering cows to graze on its grasses; wood from the gigantic trees, of ceiba and rubber and everything in between, was used to feed the engines of the boats. No longer held back by the roots of the trees and the brush, the Magdalena's banks collapsed into a muddy mess of sediment and poured into the river, which then widened and shallowed. The sheer quantity of sediment became too much for even the Magdalena to carry, and regular deposits turned into entire islands of sand that made the passage of large vessels impossible. By the 1960s, the steamboats of the Magdalena and the grandeur they brought Colombia were all but gone.

Around the same time the riverboats stopped, the armed conflict began to intensify. The river, still considered a vital thoroughfare of commerce and transport, was an asset to be seized if the country was to fall under guerrilla control. Difficulties in navigability were suddenly compounded by security concerns—boats were forced to pull over by armed groups monitoring traffic along the river and checking human and freight "inventory," or chance getting fired upon. The risks, for many, eventually became too immense to be worthwhile. Suddenly, the Magdalena was a place nobody wanted to go.

———

THE EERIE SOUND OF THE SAND MAKING ITS PRESENCE known brought about these stories of glory and decline, which I'd read with great nostalgia before setting off on my journey. I envied those travelers who wrote of the Magdalena's golden dawns on steamboat mornings, of the cacophony of monkeys and insects in its trees and the cries of manatees in its waters, because these were things I knew I would never see. In a life marked by news of slaughtered wildernesses and vanishing species, and doomed by impending climate catastrophes, I envied them just as I have long envied those lucky enough, in a world before mine, to experience the majesty of nature without feeling the crushing weight of so much loss.

Perhaps this is because there are not many entirely natural things left back home, in the sprawling suburbs of New York where I grew up, where many towns are leafy and green, yes, but also where the rivers are polluted with sewage and industrial runoff, and underground brooks are only noticed when they flood basements. Homes are lined right up against one another, coyotes are driven out of our neighborhoods because of their threat to our pets, and distant highways lull us to sleep the way oceans should. And yet my parents—doctors, scientists, both of them—long instilled in my brothers and me the idea that there is nothing more important than understanding our place in the natural world. At home in the suburbs, our connections to that world were small but clearly defined—like the arrival of the autumn winds, or the crisp smell of an impending snowfall. As kids, only every now and then would we find remnants of all the nature that once dominated our neighborhood well before we lived in it— discovering a toad hiding underneath the base of our basketball hoop after a rainstorm, or our tree sprouting a lonely nectarine; learning that the stone wall on our dead-end street marked the end of an old turkey-hunting trail back when everything was woods. Such discoveries were so rare that they were news to us; the toad quickly gained an audience of ten curious onlookers, the nectarine a legion of guards against the hungry squirrels.

In these ways, from a very young age my brothers and I learned to fall in love with the natural world. And I think that only once you have fallen in love with something can you truly not bear to see it disappear. Now it is difficult for me to wade in a river without wondering if the water is clean and free-flowing, impossible to stand atop a mountain and overlook an endless sea of trees without fearing that they might someday be bulldozed or burned. As I grew older, learning that this was also a world of deforestation and plastic pollution and climate change, any adventures in nature near or far became inextricably tied to the sense that it was being spoiled by our very hands. Could traveling to a place like Colombia—or anywhere an airplane flight away—ever justify the climate harm that my journey would ultimately (unfairly) cause the people I met, those very same people whose stories of struggles with nature I hoped to share?

———

FELIPE, AT THIS POINT, SEEMED TO HAVE LOST INTEREST in my incessant questions about the river in its natural state. "Get closer to Salchi and take a picture, so he comes out in your book."

Salchi did not care to take a picture and continued to point things out on the riverbank. To our left, the dusky, ink-colored waters of the Río Bogotá—a putrid and polluted tributary coming from the capital—flowed into the Magdalena. "Here you can already see the difference in the color of the water," Salchi said.

"It's black," Felipe observed.

"Being black isn't *always* the same as being dirty, that's a stigma we have with human beings too," his friend quipped back. "I'm dark, but I bathe myself every day. You're dark, and you bathe yourself every day too."

"So what?"

"It's the same with the Magdalena, anytime you see the Magdalena you'll see it coffee-colored. The only way to see it clear and crystalline would be to go to its source. Everywhere else, it'll be the color of coffee."

"Hmm."

At the southern end of the mouth of the Río Bogotá, we came upon a blue dump truck that was submerged up to the tops of its back tires in the fast-flowing meeting of waters. Its hopper was filled with dark, wet sand, and two men were standing barefoot atop its load, smoothing it over with metal shovels. From a long, narrow wooden canoe anchored in the water, itself nearly the length of two dump trucks, three more men were flinging the final shovel-loads of sand into the truck. These were the areneros of Girardot, the twenty or so men who spent their days digging up sand and sediment from the bed and banks of the river to sell to cement factories. The oldest among them was in his sixties; the youngest was just fifteen years old. Many worked wearing long-sleeved soccer jerseys—from the red, yellow, and blue of Colombia's national team to the stripes of Borussia Dortmund and Barcelona—and long pants, which were soaking wet and heavy from hours spent waist-deep in the water.

"We start each day at four thirty in the morning and work until around one or two in the afternoon, depending on how much sand people are looking for," one of the areneros, named Luis, told me later in the day from a muddied spot on the river's edge. Several men were milling about, waiting for food that was being prepared by the only woman in sight, who was working in a kitchen shack farther uphill.

There was never a shortage of sand to be harvested, definitely not these days. Luis pointed to a sandbar in the river, called Isla del Sol—a barren, immense sandbar in the middle of the river, nearly half a mile across the way. When there was drought, Luis said, the river got so low that they could bring trucks all the way out, and there was less of a risk. At the present moment, the swiftly moving current made things more difficult. "When the river is this way, it's dangerous," he said. "If we're in a canoe that's particularly full, we could sink, lose the motor, the boat, even drown."

I asked Luis to take me out in his boat to the Isla del Sol, where I could see several waist-deep men shoveling beside another anchored canoe. Photos in tourist pamphlets showed this sunny sandbar packed with people sitting under colorful umbrellas, yet this seemed to me like a miserable place to have a vacation—sunbathing while the sand diggers toiled just feet away. The men, surefooted in the turbulent waters, lifted heavy clumps of water and mud from the riverbed onto their boat. "It's a generational thing, sons after sons after sons working on the river . . ." Luis trailed off, leaving out the most important detail: their forefathers indeed worked on the river, but as fishermen and as boat captains. Now, the sons and grandsons were condemned to this far-less-glorious life of digging the very sand and sediment that both powered and destroyed their ancestors' livelihoods just a century earlier.

We beached ourselves in the shallows beside the sandbar, and Luis directed me to wade quickly to higher ground. I stepped out of the boat to find the water warm and unnaturally silky, and I could feel the sediment dissolved in its current. But the mushy riverbed was far too soft, almost like quicksand, and I immediately found myself sinking to my knees and soaking my rolled-up pants. One of the shoveling men laughed at my discomfort; this, for them, was a regular occurrence, toiling in the murky waters, in the thick, hot air, under a sky so cloudy that at any given moment it could open and erupt with a powerful rain that would at once wash them away and easily return to the river the quantity of sediment they'd spent the day excavating, and more.

———

"THE BRIDGES AND HIGHWAYS CUT ACROSS THE RIVER, and the days of navigation were finished," Captain Rozo was known to have said of his career. The legendary boat pilot, like many of his counterparts, was eventually forced out of the transportation business—though for Girardot, relative to towns downriver with direct links to the coast, such a death came rather early. Even during the days of glory there were signals of the darker future that lay ahead. In 1925, construction began on a highway linking Girardot with other towns along the Magdalena, and by 1950, the yellow Ospina Pérez Bridge was finished, sealing Rozo's fate—for the most part, his boats remained vacant after that, waiting only to shuttle day-trippers to and from the Isla del Sol.

It was a devastating loss for a man whose entire dream in life was to be a riverboat captain. To the few who knew him well, it became clear that he would not get over the loss of the Magdalena, the river of his boyhood, for the rest of his days. "Perhaps Captain Rozo has decided to die near the river, just as one day he decided to marry it," observed the Colombian writer Juan Leonel Giraldo, while Captain Rozo was still alive, in his essay "Some People of the River." "In the meantime, he and his men struggle to hold on to the dream that the days of the past will return, and that they will someday work on the Magdalena once more."

Their dream, of course, never did come true. A few months before Captain Rozo eventually did die, in the late 1980s, his family sold the company to Salchi's father, who spent decades trying to revive river transport out of Girardot's wharf, to little avail. All that attracted people seemed to be the chance to vacation atop the Isla del Sol. In 2016, Salchi's father threw himself off of a bridge into the Magdalena's waters. After an exhaustive, days-long search, his body was found floating between Ambalema and Cambao, not far from where Captain Rozo's passengers used to disembark and continue their downriver journeys.

Salchi runs La Barca del Capitán Rozo these days. A lonely job, indeed, but one that has in many ways required the same intrinsic love for these waters that got Captain Rozo started in the first place. Salchi, like his father and Rafael Rozo before him, has a sort of instinctive knowledge of the Magdalena, having traveled it many times between Neiva and Barrancabermeja, farther north.

"This river," Salchi said to me as we were cruising back to the silent wharf populated with empty boats, "there's something special about it. It teaches you things, every day it teaches you. Every day the river changes. You can never say you know the Magdalena."

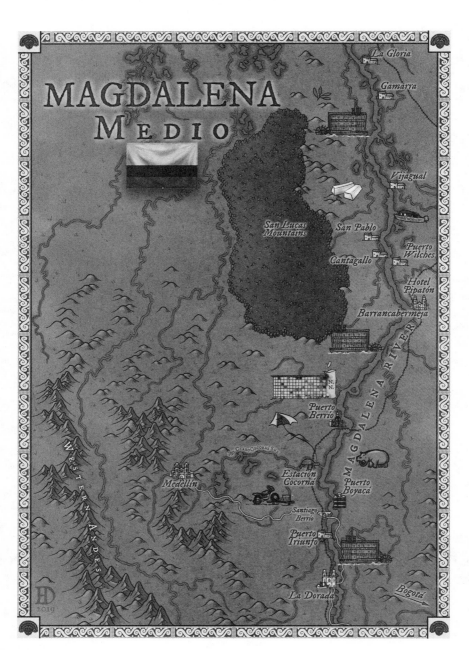

PART TWO

Magdalena Medio

Mid-Magdalena

5

The Hippopotamuses of Pablo Escobar

THE MAGDALENA MEDIO, OR THE MID-MAGDALENA VALLEY, spans more than ten thousand square miles on either side of the river. The landscape is vast and varied, marked at once by tremendous biodiversity—still-forested mountains, and wetlands critical for spawning wildlife—and stripped expanses of farmland and pastures where dense, humid jungles no longer remain.

Nearly a million people live here, in settlements spread out across the land. Most of the larger towns are situated directly on the banks of the Magdalena, following one after another along the river's northward course like a line of leafcutter ants. Elsewhere, tiny agrarian villages with spellbinding names like El Delirio (Delirium) look like small specks in the grass amid the unwavering countryside.

For decades, the Magdalena Medio was also a major theater for the violence that came to so harshly define the world's perception of

Colombia in the late twentieth century—when sporadic raids by vicious paramilitary squads and guerrilla factions led to frequent massacres and disappearances. Many people say it was this place, the true Colombian heartland, that coined one of the Río Magdalena's many nicknames: River of Blood.

Famously, of course, just fifteen miles west of the river in the southern part of the Magdalena Medio, the notorious drug kingpin Pablo Escobar owned a sprawling country estate known as the Hacienda Nápoles. In 1978, he bought the land—more than three thousand hectares in his home department of Antioquia, mainly flat pastures with a few hills—and immediately began making the place his own. This included—in addition to the construction of dozens of residential buildings, several swimming pools, and a landing strip— the importation of exotic animals from Africa. His private zoo of giraffes, rhinoceroses, ostriches, and hippopotamuses was completed in the late 1980s, a source of entertainment for Escobar and his guests, as well as a grandiose show of wealth and power by the host.

In 1993, one day after turning forty-four, Escobar was shot dead by the Colombian police in Medellín, his hometown, and his estate in the valley of the Magdalena River fell into disarray. Control of the buildings was assumed by the government, which could not afford the costs of maintaining the animals and sent them to domestic and international zoos. The only ones too enormous to be transported were the four hippopotamuses, who eventually fled the confines of their enclosures and escaped into several nearby lakes. There, they began to reproduce, thriving in the wet, tropical climate and taking advantage of the vast tracts of undeveloped land of the Magdalena Medio. Approximately one hundred hippopotamuses are now thought to inhabit a roughly eight-hundred-square-mile stretch of the extensive valley, according to modeled estimates of population growth. The only known wild population living outside of Africa, the hippopotamuses have been definitively sighted in rural hamlets as far as Cimitarra, nearly fifty miles away on the eastern side of the Magdalena, and in towns as close as Puerto Triunfo—less than ten miles from Escobar's old Hacienda—wandering through the streets to the fascination of onlookers. In early 2020, fishermen reported seeing what they presumed to be a hippopotamus near the river port of Magangué, far to the north; if confirmed, it would mean that the animals have spread some two hundred miles downriver.

More than a decade ago, two hippopotamuses, one male and one female, found their way into the Río Claro Cocorná Sur, a gentle tributary whose course meanders not far from the boundaries of the old Hacienda Nápoles. Wallowing in the shallows and gorging themselves on the abundant grasses and shrubs of the wetlands along its banks, the animals made their way east down the river, until they reached its confluence with the great Magdalena. The point where the Río Claro Cocorná Sur meets the Río Magdalena is far enough from any town to make for a wide, quiet stretch of water where the hippopotamuses could live relatively unbothered—so they stayed. Recently, they gave birth to a child, making three. The female was thought to be pregnant with another. I had heard that these particular Magdalena River hippos were becoming aggressive, causing some trouble with the handful of local fishermen who live near the waters of the confluence, so I decided to see for myself. I would have to make my way to Estación Cocorná, the closest village to the confluence, on the banks not of the Magdalena but of the Río Claro Cocorná Sur.

Estación Cocorná barely registers on most maps. One of the Magdalena Medio's specks in the grass.

———

THE MOTOBALINERA IS PERHAPS THE MOST CURIOUS form of transportation in all of Colombia, no small feat in a country where rickety motorcycles are driven at breakneck speeds along narrow jungle trails of roots and stones, and sparkling new cable car systems connect the poorest slums of its largest cities. Known in some regions as brujita, or "little witch," because of the eerie whirring sound it makes as it flashes by, the motobalinera consists of a wooden platform fixed with rail wheels, propelled by a motorcycle along a single line of railroad track. In many cases, the railroad tracks are completely abandoned—while on other rarer occasions, like this one, the solitary freight train still thunders through, without much regard at all for any semblance of a timetable that may exist. It goes without saying that the freight train does not cede passage to the motobalinera; in these situations, passengers must be prepared to jump.

I first found the motobalinera that would take me to Estación Cocorná at around 8:00 p.m. in the dark, beneath the overpass of the roaring Medellín–Bogotá highway. I had established a personal rule that I would not travel at night, arriving in new spots along the river only under the protection of daylight. But on my way to Estación Cocorná, a combination of delays—rain, treacherous road conditions, an uncharacteristically slow bus driver—forced me to break this rule for the first time. I anxiously watched out the dirt-smudged window of the bus as the sun disappeared behind a grassy hill, and an older woman sitting next to me took note of my concern.

"Where are you getting off, mijo?" she asked, placing her hand gently on my arm. She looked to be in her sixties.

"A place called Santiago Berrío," I replied. "Will you tell me when we get there?"

"Santiago Berrío ..." Her voice trailed off, and she raised her eyebrows. She thought to herself for a moment. "Well, now, I do not know where that is. I think you must mean *Puerto* Berrío. You must change buses at Puerto Triunfo, it is another three hours away ..."

"No, no, *Santiago* Berrío," I corrected her. "I am looking for a motobalinera to Estación Cocorná."

"Ahhh." Remembering, at last, that such a place existed, she nodded. "Santiago Berrío, yes, it's just up ahead. But be careful, mijo, it's not safe at this time of night." She gave me her card, which said she was a public defense lawyer. "Anything you need ..." My wandering mind returned to the hazy anxiety of what could go wrong on country roads after dark.

I was extra alert when I stepped off the bus in Santiago Berrío, which was indeed a town that is easy to forget, nothing more than a cluster of homes and a small playground just beside the highway. The action was centered along the road, with people taking advantage of the speed bumps that slowed passing traffic. Tire repair shops, small restaurants, and rest stops were illuminated by the dull orange light of just a few streetlamps. Each place had its own loudspeaker, and as the simultaneous thump of several different reggaeton songs charged the corridor, it almost seemed a competition as to who could play louder music to attract customers. Men and women hawked warm cheese and pastries from plastic Tupperware containers—if they were lucky, they sold one piece at a time through the small openings of bus windows in exchange for a handful of coins.

A group of these food sellers surrounded me the moment the bus pulled away, and my fear of the place—as rational or irrational as it may have been—led me to rudely push past them in search of the railroad track, which I eventually found after descending a muddy staircase that led to the underpass. I waited for several minutes beside the entrance to the tunnel, standing in a patch of grass along the single stitch of track leading into the darkness on either side. It was amazing how much quieter it was just a few feet below the highway. A frog croaked every now and then, adding some variety to the shrill, unbroken whistle of the cicadas that had arrived with the night. Eventually, a bright light became visible farther down the track, and I realized something was approaching. As the light grew, it came accompanied by a whirring sound. *Brujita*, I thought. Little witch.

The motobalinera was nearly full by the time it got to me at Santiago Berrío. It was on its way back to Estación Cocorná from Puerto Triunfo, the municipal seat, and the wooden platform of the vehicle was occupied by six members of a family sitting in red and white plastic chairs. Their faces were dark in the dim light, and they all stepped off the platform for the driver, Jorge, to unstack and rearrange some of the chairs so I could have a seat. Once we were all settled, the driver revved the back wheel of the motorcycle—the front wheel had been removed, the moto frame secured to the wooden platform—and we set off. The motobalinera must not have been moving faster than fifteen miles per hour, but the wind in our faces and the buzz of the metal wheels on rails beneath our feet was nothing short of exhilarat-

ing. We raced—or so it felt—north through the pitch-black countryside, and only by the light of the moon were we able to make out
the silhouettes of the long, verdant plains strewn with small grassy
mounds and slumbering cows on either side of our route. We crossed
a bridge over a small creek, and the familiar railroad smell of creosote
was fresh in the air. For a second, I felt as if I were back home, com-
muting on some eight-car behemoth into New York's Grand Central
Terminal. But then an eagle jetted off from a bush, a lazy dog scampered at the very last second from his trackside nap—scared even by
us, for the motobalinera was the behemoth here. Several miles to our
right, not visible even during the daytime from this inland stretch of
tracks, the Magdalena flowed parallel to our route.

The darkness was occasionally pierced by bursts of light. Fire-
flies blinked in the grass beside the tracks, emitting unexpected white
flashes instead of yellow ones. To the west, the faraway mountains of
the Central Cordillera were now and again lit up by flares of lightning, the thunder too distant to be heard. We passed one-room farmhouses of wooden planks and black tarps, the faces of the people who
lived there illuminated only by candlelight. In Estación Pita, the only
sizable settlement (of around a dozen visible homes) between Santiago Berrío and Estación Cocorná, a well-lit soccer field sent a wide
beam into the starry sky.

Upon entering the limits of Estación Cocorná, we encountered
cargo coming toward us on the track. Three young men were wheel-
ing, by hand, a rail cart stacked with bags of gravel. Generally, right-
of-way is a cordial affair: between oncoming motobalineras, the party
with fewer passengers would have to disembark and lift the entire apparatus off the track for the other to pass. Several days later, a moto-

balinera I was on would come up behind a man using an oar to "row" his makeshift, engineless platform along the tracks; despite the fact that his cart carried a heavy load of bananas, we were moving in the same direction, so he had to let us pass. But in the face of the gravel movers, Jorge killed the motorcycle engine, and we pushed back several hundred feet until they arrived at their destination. We watched as they hoisted the very heavy bags off the cart, one by one, and dumped them onto an already existing pile of gravel on a fenced-in trackside property. Then, they lifted their empty cart off the tracks, and we were able to continue on our way, finally reaching the town center at around nine o'clock at night.

———

THE EXPEDITION WOULD COMMENCE AT DAWN. THE riverboat—a colorful, motorized launch—could fit six of us, plus a motorman and his assistant. The team was a mixture of local community leaders and regional environmental scientists. David Echeverri López, who'd organized the outing, was a young biologist at CORNARE (a regional environmental agency) in charge of its efforts to deal with the hippopotamuses. Saulo Hoyos was a gruff, retired environmental scientist and an eminent figure when it came to the Magdalena River—he claimed to have floated from here all the way down to the river's mouth on a wooden raft several times, giving him an intimate understanding of its every twist and turn. David and Saulo could not have been more opposite in personality: David was a soft-spoken man who chose his words sparingly, while Saulo was more bombastic, with a bit of a temper. But both were educated men with a deep understanding and appreciation for the natural world around them, or whatever was still left of it. They had been colleagues for many years and were the closest of friends.

Isabel "Chava" Romero was born in 1961 in a fishing shack on an island of the Magdalena River, not far from the shores of Puerto Triunfo, the nearby municipal seat. In the 1970s, after her parents separated, she came with her father to Estación Cocorná, one of the many towns centered around now-abandoned train stations, where she's lived ever since. Isabel learned to read and write when she was thirty-five; after that, she received a university degree, and as part of her studies, she created a community sanctuary for the Magdalena River turtle (*Podocnemis lewyana*), endemic only to a few river basins in northern Colombia and critically endangered because of uncontrolled habitat loss, overharvesting of its eggs, and river contamination over the course of the past century. She has become another of Colombia's many intrepid social leaders, an enthusiastic conservationist who, with hardly any financial resources, regularly leads groups of locals on educational riverboat trips to collect and safeguard turtle eggs and release the hatchlings back into the wild several months later. The boat was hers, captained by her son Alvarito—a jovial, bleary-eyed obese man of thirty-five—and his assistant, Isabel's nephew Daniel, a twenty-three-year-old with a kind smile. Two women from the environmental protection office in Puerto Triunfo, named Gloria and (fittingly) Magdalena, rounded out the group.

The hippopotamuses were supposedly active at all hours of the day. The early start wasn't about that, David told me, but about the sun: once it reached a certain height in the sky, the heat would become unbearable on the water. After a breakfast of eggs and arepas (Saulo ate a cold slab of grilled meat) on Isabel's patio, which extended to the riverfront, we piled into the boat and pushed off.

We motored peacefully downstream for several minutes; Daniel, sitting atop the bow, was Alvarito's eyes for the route ahead. He periodically pointed down toward either side of the boat, indicating some sort of obstacle necessitating a direction change—a sunken tree or fallen branch—or visibly shallow water that required us to drift motorless for a few seconds. This was the dry season, and though the water level was lower, it was glassy and easy to see its depth to the sandy bottom.

The rising sun gave light to river turtles slipping off logs and red howler monkeys stirring in the guadua trees. Isabel excitedly pointed out each river turtle, while Saulo identified every other species with the confidence and precision of a nature guidebook. Cocoi herons— white-necked birds with gray wings, orange beaks, and blue-ringed eyes—took flight from their roosts at the last possible second of our approach, while the great egrets remained steadfast in their perches, following us with side-eyed glances until we were out of sight. Umbrellalike ceiba trees, with their enormous trunks, towered over the river as we motored past. The tall oil pumpjacks, blue and rusted nonanimal specimens that stood silently and assertively out of place along the riverbank, were a close second in height as a stark reminder of the oil-rich lands of the Magdalena Medio, some of the most productive in Colombia.

Cows trundled in groups along the pastureland shores. "It's as if, for the cattle ranchers, trees are the enemy," Saulo said, shaking his head. He pointed out the erosion on the edges of the river and told me I would see it on an even greater scale as I continued north along the Magdalena. The land seemed to be ripped from the shore in some places, a cross-section of the soil layers visible beneath the grassy surface. Along healthier stretches of land, Saulo showed me, species of leguminous trees had not been removed, and their strong roots continued to hold the soil together despite the current.

We neared the meeting of the rivers after about an hour of motoring downstream. David pointed out a clearing across from a cluster of crumbling homes. "This is where the hippos sometimes come out to eat the grass," he said, "like cows."

Finally, we curved left around a bend, and there it was. "Welcome to the Río Magdalena!" Isabel rubbed my shoulder, a proud smile on her face. "The most beautiful, the most important in all of Colombia!"

Long gone were the dark coffee-colored rapids of Quinchana, the muddy waters of Girardot and Neiva, the hiss of sediment, and the black gully of the Río Bogotá. In the Magdalena Medio, the river looked more like the one described in the stories—half a mile wide, glassy and calm, with flat expanses of land lining its shores.

We crossed the line of current that marked the larger river's absorption of its tributary, our wooden boat jolted by the swift change in undertow. Suddenly I was lucid, silently alert to the possibility of hippopotamuses in our midst. We had entered the small patch of river where they had taken up residence. *There!* I thought to myself, several times in a row, with every upwelling bubble beside the boat. Each time, I was wrong—fooled by a tree trunk, a small rapid, a pile of dirt on the shore. I was hopeful; in fact, it was so common to run into the animals on this stretch of the river, David assured me on the phone before I arrived, that he'd never *not* seen one during a trip on the water. That was part of the problem.

Downriver, we approached an inconspicuous lean-to on the western bank, just before the river curved around a bend and out of sight. It was a cambuche, one of the many simple riverside fishing huts found along the Magdalena, the kind where Isabel was born. This one was held up by bamboo shoots and shaded by a roof of palm fronds; a solitary dog watched over the small strip of sand in front of it and began barking furiously as we neared the shore. According to Isabel, an elderly fisherman had been living there for decades, spending his days catching fish from his wooden canoe and harvesting plantains on a nearby river island. His real name was Ederardo Pérez, but everyone knew him affectionately as Don Pira. Don Pira emerged from the trees behind his cambuche as our boat slid onto its resting place in the sand. He had a bushy mustache and wore a blue baseball cap.

"Hola, Don Pira!" Isabel called out to him.

He raised his arm in acknowledgment. "Chava!" It impressed me that they seemed to know each other quite well, despite living so far apart.

Don Pira showed us his cambuche. A hammock hung low between two wooden poles; above it, just beneath the palm fronds, was a platform where he slept on a thin mattress, accessed each night by climbing another wooden log that lay slanted against it like a ladder. Behind the cambuche, farther inland among the trees, was a larger, enclosed structure, whose wooden walls were collecting moss. This was where he cooked and cleaned.

It didn't take long for him to tell us that he'd had a run-in with one of the hippopotamuses just a day earlier. "The son of a bitch almost killed me out on the island," he said, pointing to a green, rather large landmass in front of us that looked like the eastern bank of the river but was actually an island blocking our view of the other side. There, Don Pira told us, he was picking his plantains when he heard a wheezing noise and realized it was one of the hippos approaching.

"I had to ditch the plantains and just start running," he said, proceeding to describe how he took off sprinting, barefoot, in a desperate attempt to reach his canoe. "I ran into a wooden log and got this splinter, look at this." He picked up a shard of split wood, several inches long, that had apparently been lodged in the sole of his foot. "This thing was in so deep that I couldn't get it out with my fingernails. I had to come back here and use pliers."

"Are the hippos here usually very aggressive?" I asked. I remembered hearing once that hippopotamuses were the deadliest animals in Africa when it came to human attacks.

"Yes, mostly the female. The female will follow you. You get to an area and she's there, coming closer to flip the canoe or come up out of the water. She's dangerous."

"Do they ever come up here, to your house?"

"No, just out there on the island." He pointed again to the brown sands of the island out front. "Time to stop talking about it. Instead, put together a group and get rid of them. They're going to kill someone."

David, ever selective with his words, looked down at the ground as he listened quietly to Don Pira's account. Despite Don Pira's impassioned pleas, David later told me, the process of removing the animals would not be an easy one. In 2009, a multiday hunt culminated in the killing of Pepe, one of the four original hippopotamuses imported by Escobar, after he was sighted roaming the streets of the town of Puerto Berrío. But a leaked photo of sixteen Colombian army soldiers posing sternly with Pepe's corpse—the animal's moist flesh glinting in the low light, as if it were a trophy—caused public outcry and resulted in a judge declaring it illegal to kill hippopotamuses in Colombia. It took me a while to let the irony of such a ruling sink in—that for all the poaching, species trafficking, and overall ecological extermination that goes on in the world's second-most biodiverse country, the plight of the invasive but charismatic hippopotamus was what brought about swift court-ordered protection.

Many groups have advocated relocating the hippos to zoos, where they can be better controlled; castrating some of the males is also on the table. But massive costs—thousands of dollars per animal—and the dangers of working with hippos make for a significant logistical challenge. And some researchers are convinced that because of an absence of natural predators and diseases that keep the reproduction rates of African hippos in check, such strategies might not be enough.

"The problem is that the population keeps growing and growing," David told me. "The behavior of these animals makes dealing with them a challenge for even the most experienced professionals. They are massive animals who will resist."

The majority of the hundred or so animals believed to exist today live in the vicinity of the old Hacienda Nápoles, now a theme park where families with children can buy tickets to gleefully observe the hippos wallowing in a series of lakes. A small number of scientists have suggested potential benefits to having hippopotamuses in Colombia, including as a backup supply to help re-wild more vulnerable African hippo populations. But local biologists' biggest worry, according to David, is the uncontrolled spread of the animals that become lost in the no-man's-land of the Magdalena Medio—territorial disputes, he said, often result in long migrations like the one that saw the two animals follow the Río Claro Cocorná Sur all the way to the Magdalena. That's when they could pose a serious threat to the surrounding ecosystem by displacing endangered or endemic fauna—like manatees and river turtles—and by changing the chemical makeup of rivers and wetlands with their waste. It's also when people like Don Pira can get hurt.

And yet, the invasive hippos of Colombia have long lent themselves to cartoonish stories and clickbait headlines around the world, almost seen as a joke for readers removed from their complex social and ecological consequences. "You have to take into account all that it entails for a community to have one of these animals around," David told me. "What may seem like a funny story to some people is a very dangerous situation for others."

As I poked around Don Pira's cambuche, I overheard one of the other local environmental workers, the woman named Magdalena, pleading with the fisherman to take caution around the hippos. "Don't throw your fishing net anywhere near them," she instructed, her hands clasped. "They are dangerous. Be careful."

But for Don Pira, hippopotamuses or not, fishing is a necessary risk. Standing beside his cambuche earlier, he'd told me that due to declining fish numbers and sizes, many people along the river were suffering. "There's a lot of contamination in the river, and too many people fishing, poor people, so there's very little fish left," he said. "We're hungry."

After Magdalena gave Don Pira her parting advice, Saulo hurriedly ushered us back into the boat. He was frustrated that we had taken this long, for he'd spotted another fisherman far off in the distance, back in the direction where we came from, and wanted to ask him if he'd seen the hippopotamuses earlier in the morning. We said goodbye to Don Pira and motored toward the next fisherman. He was relaxing on the water in his canoe, which he'd tied to a root on the shore to prevent the current from carrying him downstream. The boat was colorful and looked like it could have been assembled in Neiva by Delfín Borrero. The shade of some low-hanging fruit trees shielded him from the sun, which grew fiercer by the minute.

He pointed us to a nearby, partially submerged log where he'd seen a hippopotamus surface just minutes earlier. Saulo grunted. We'd missed it.

"There!" David said suddenly, still hushed in volume, pointing to a large ball-shaped object that had emerged still and unwavering among the swiftly moving waters. The hippopotamus's head could have passed as a plastic replica had it not been for its eyes, which followed us as we made a quick, sweeping pass with the boat. Its ears flicked back occasionally, sending drops of water flying behind it. Several days later, a few of us would return on another excursion to see the male and the female standing together in the shallows, sunning their corpulent backs. That time, our attempt at a much closer pass was dangerously unsuccessful: we were only a few yards from the enormous animals when the boat's motor, trying to race through the shallow waters of the sedimented river, got stuck in the mud and died. Their calf likely close by, the hippopotamuses stared at us with unrelenting gazes.

We panicked. "Are they coming closer?" Alvarito yelled, frantically trying to restart the engine. One of the hippos turned toward us and silently yawned, baring its thick teeth dripping with saliva.

I screamed, but nobody heard me because at that moment the motor roared back to life. We sped away as quickly as we could.

But now, racing past our first sighting, we were giddy—and looking back on it, we weren't acting all that differently from the tourists at Escobar's old Hacienda. "Esooo! Epaaa!" Alvarito, Daniel, and Isabel laughed loudly and cheered. Magdalena, Gloria, and I took photos. Even Saulo smiled. The only one who did not react was David—he just sat there, gazing quietly at the lingering hippopotamus as the boat flew past. We did not stop in our escape from the Magdalena River to the calmer tributary that would eventually take us back to Estación Cocorná.

6

Four Days in
Estación Cocorná

IN ESTACIÓN COCORNÁ THE TEMPERATURES REGULARLY
soared past ninety-five degrees, and the air was thick with humidity
and the lingering smell of the jungle. People spent their entire days outside, for work and for rest—even at night, it was too hot in their small,
single-level homes. During the afternoons, they sat on concrete stoops,
in shaded rocking chairs, or in doorways with loud metal fans whirring, waiting for the sun to dip behind the low hills outside town. It was
such a cruel heat, I think, that it is impossible to understand without
experiencing—how it drains every ounce of strength from your body
from the moment you rise in the morning until you're able to finally fall
asleep in the darkness. Sometimes at night I was lucky, and the lightning we watched crackling silently over the mountains far to the west
would eventually reach us, bringing downpours that cooled the concrete
homes and metal roofs like sizzling pans beneath a cold tap.

I spent a total of four days in the village. David and Saulo, who'd made their way into town only for our early-morning hippo expedition, left almost as soon as it was finished. I was under the care of Isabel and her family—Alvarito, the boat captain, also a fisherman and a moto-taxi driver; her nephew Daniel, the boat assistant; and her husband, Álvaro Sr., an older man with a bushy mustache, who rarely left the seclusion of the house. The group was rounded out by giddy children and neighbors who weren't all related to Isabel but acted as her extended family, running barefoot across the hot dirt floor of her patio toward the relief of the cool waters of the river Cocorná. There, on the riverbank, they sat in the shade of a large rubber tree, beneath its colossal trunk and green leaves faded yellow. After the sun went down in the evenings, they would move their plastic chairs to the street, where they ate their dinner while listening to accordion music and chatting with neighbors.

"When a place is warm, the people are warm, too," I wrote in my journal of the life of the campesinos, the people of Colombia's countryside. I thought of life back home and how cold it was, how after work each day we locked ourselves in our houses and apartments and watched television until we went to bed. But for all of the days I stayed in Estación Cocorná, it never felt this way. I was enchanted by the thought of a life outside, in this all-encompassing warmth—of a life lived forever in the company of family and friends.

Later, I wondered if this was entirely true. Estación Cocorná, though only an hour's motobalinera ride from the nearest major town, also felt severely isolated—and because of that, its residents suffered from great hardship and solitude. All too often their meals consisted of slimy river fish, smaller by the year, fried whole and then picked to the bone. The culture of sitting and socializing by day and by night was, for many, an unfortunate consequence of not having any work. Most villagers' jobs were centered around informal resource extraction: fishing, harvesting sediment from the riverbed, and gathering wild limes. None of those things were particularly lucrative. Those who had what was considered more "formal" employment worked in oil fields or on the pastures of wealthy landowners from cities like Medellín, tending to the brown and white cows and sleeping in shacks with dirt floors along the railroad track. At night, clouds of smoke from the wood-burning stoves billowed through the cracks in the walls, creating the illusion that the huts were burning up from the inside.

Isabel and her family were the only ones I'd heard of who were working in tourism, let alone ecotourism—they maintained the place where I was staying, a small guesthouse down the road with several beds in cell-like quarters that altogether had the ventilation of a cigar box. But tourists hardly ever came to Estación Cocorná. One morning, I woke up surprised to hear the rumble of several jeeps passing by my window. They were transporting a group of light-skinned Medellín day-trippers who had come for a float down the river Cocorná in large inner tubes. Led by a young tour operator, Camilo Toro, who wore a Boston Red Sox baseball cap and spoke perfect English, the tourists were as surprised to see me as I was to see them. After several sleepless nights in the insufferable heat, I hated myself for feeling relieved that outsiders had come, because they reminded me of an unspoken sense of freedom and privilege that we shared—the sense that, unlike the people who lived here, we could always leave. This made me deeply uncomfortable. It didn't seem immediately clear whether Isabel would be making any money from their visit, either (Camilo's family owned the only large home in the village, a luxurious, air-conditioned cabin just past Isabel's place along the riverbank, and had all of the tour components ready themselves), but she followed them around with glee as they prepared to take a boat upriver to the launch point for their float back down. Her main project in town, of course, was the turtle sanctuary, and she relied on visitors to spread the word. So, in the early morning before they arrived, she'd gone to the sanctuary, collected more than twenty black baby turtles that had hatched in an incubator after the last nesting season, and prepared them in a large blue bucket for their imminent release into the river.

We followed the day-trippers' two motorized boats upriver. Brown eagles with white-tipped wings flapped and soared over the river ahead of us, often carrying small fish in their claws. We passed a towering 122-year-old ceiba tree, which Isabel said was the tallest tree in the area. Its nickname was "The Girlfriend of Cocorná." At one point, we motored beneath two thick wire lines stretching across the river, several hundred feet apart from each other. "So that the howler monkeys can cross!" Isabel announced with pride. A community accomplishment. The turtles, piled atop one another in the bucket, were restless in their excited scraping, and I constantly readjusted the giant elephant-ear leaf that Isabel had placed over them to keep them shielded from the sun.

After a few minutes, all of the boats stopped at a wide river beach. We waded through the warm, shallow water onto the shore, and Isabel cradled the bucket like it was a small child. The tourists shot each other uneasy glances, not sure of what was happening. When she pulled out the first baby turtle, no more than six inches long, the crowd gasped, and the children jumped with excitement. She placed the turtle on the ground, and it immediately began scrambling over the rocky sand toward the waterline.

A woman screamed. Her hungry dog, a shaggy beast, began charging in the direction of the hatchling. The turtle, oblivious to it all, wouldn't have ever reached the water if the dog hadn't been tackled by its owner at the very last moment.

With the dog tied up, all of the turtles were successfully released under Isabel's watch. It was now a common sight along the banks of the Cocorná: dozens of the tiny black reptiles scurrying into the water away from the outstretched arms of people, mainly children. Colombians reclaiming their nature, as Isabel saw it. What started out as a personal passion ended up having real impact—despite still-sparse funds—and turtle sightings are steadily becoming more common along the river.

"When I was seventeen or eighteen there were so many turtles ... so many!" Alvarito would say to me a few days later. "Now, they're coming back. One day my children will see them again like that, and that's thanks to Mamá."

The isolation of a town like this one also meant that a considerable amount of improvisation was necessary in order to get by. Alvarito served as a sort of multipurpose handyman for the village—I first realized this when, one morning, he proudly instructed me to smell what was inside a gasoline canister he was carrying. After I gagged and recoiled at the rancid odor, he told me it was a drink called chicha—alcohol homemade from fermented pineapple skins.

"One year in the making!" he announced. "And tonight, we will drink it together." I politely declined.

Another day, I was watching as he built a "custom lightbulb"—by pulling two different lightbulbs apart and putting the pieces together to make a new one—when Aicardo, an older man in the village, came by gently cradling a light-brown cat that needed "surgery." The cat had been sterilized earlier in the week, they told me, and needed the stitches removed from its right thigh. I asked if the sterilization occurred in a clinic in Puerto Triunfo. Alvarito shook his head with a grin.

"You're looking at the veterinarian of Estación Cocorná!" he said, pulling out a razor blade.

"Where are you going to do it?" I asked, immediately regretting the question.

"Right here!" Alvarito and Aicardo pinned down the cat on the same blue plastic table where we'd been eating all of our meals. Aicardo kept a strong grip on the cat's neck and behind, rendering it immobile, while Alvarito—without hesitating—used the blade to cut the stitches from the animal's leg, one by one. At one point, out of desperation, it clawed at Aicardo and tried to bite Alvarito, briefly regaining some control before Aicardo slammed its head down once more. Small drops of blood trickled from its leg onto the table and then down onto the dirt floor.

As soon as the procedure was finished, Aicardo lifted his hands and liberated the cat, who sprang up from the table and onto the ground. "Pobrecito," he said quietly, the cat meowing as it limped away.

———

"WHEN I WAS SEVEN YEARS OLD, I STARTED FISHING AND I started smoking," said Aurelio Delgado Calderón, eighty-eight years old, as he sat in the shade outside the main convenience store in Estación Cocorná with a cigarette between his fingers. He flashed me a toothless smile. "I'm still doing both."

I made it a point in every town I visited along the Magdalena to seek out its oldest residents, who could look at the river and see all that it once was. Aurelio, who'd been living in this sleepy riverside village for more than seventy years, was one of those people. "The Magdalena, father of waters, one of the great rivers of the world, was only an illusion of memory," Gabriel García Márquez wrote in his 1985 novel *Love in the Time of Cholera*. For Aurelio, whose entire life took place in a world tied to the Magdalena, that memory was peace.

Born in the village of Cambao, south of here on the river's eastern edge, Aurelio recalled moving to Estación Cocorná with his wife and two children in 1948, back when there couldn't have been more than three hundred homes in town, all of them congregated around the train track. The town was built and named for its large stone train station, which served the passenger lines that originated in the northern Caribbean port city of Santa Marta and ran south through the country, roughly parallel to the Magdalena's course. The trains, much like the riverboats, were slow-moving but luxurious affairs. Elegant passengers in first class wore suits and gowns and ate meals with wine in special dining cars—and whenever a train arrived in town, the townspeople would flood the tracks beside the station in jubilation and excitement, many of them hoping to sell travelers refreshments and supplies for the five-hundred-mile, multiday trip.

"There used to be so much going on here," Aurelio told me, as we looked out on a quiet plaza that was now equipped with lights, soccer goals and basketball hoops without nets, and tall, empty bleachers for spectators. The town was more vibrant back then, he said, bustling with merchants carrying yucca and corn from the looming mountains of Antioquia to the west and fresh limes from nearby riverbanks for loading onto the trains. The river ran deep, the fishing was good. "It was paradise," Aurelio said. "But the violence ended it all."

The death of the navigable Magdalena meant an end to the transport of passengers along the entire corridor soon afterward— and when the steamboats and trains stopped running, and armed groups took over, living along the river didn't have many advantages anymore. While a freight train still rumbles through town every few weeks or so, hauling 91 million annual tons of coffee, oil, and other goods between the interior and the coast, the train station was abandoned, and people stopped coming to Estación Cocorná altogether. Right around the same time, extreme right-wing paramilitaries began challenging the Marxist guerrillas in a proxy war that consumed the countryside.

The guerrillas, fighting against the Colombian government supposedly in the name of wealth redistribution for the country's landless poor, made a major point of kidnapping wealthy landowners for ransom in order to fund their activities. And in the 1970s and '80s, as the drug trade began to make more money than cartel bosses knew what to do with, traffickers began buying land in order to launder their riches. With support from wealthy ranchers, representatives from U.S. oil companies, and anyone else who shared their interests in beating back the guerrillas, the traffickers turned landowners funded the creation of private militias to defend their assets.

Among the earliest of these paramilitary militias was perhaps the most terrifying of them all: the vigilante group Muerte a Secuestradores (MAS), or "Death to Kidnappers." In the span of its first six months in 1982, MAS was believed to have murdered eighty people and caused the displacement of five hundred more, warning their intended victims by note in their homes to "leave or die." Backed by seemingly endless drug money, and forging close ties with the Colombian military and prominent conservative Colombian politicians, the paramilitaries only expanded their reign of terror from there: indeed, since the start of the conflict, paramilitary groups have been accused of killing nearly one hundred thousand people, many of them civilians, and committing a vast array of human rights violations.

With so many different armed groups vying for control of the region, by the 1980s, most townspeople in Estación Cocorná were living under a vow of silence—people kept opinions to themselves, so long as they didn't want any trouble. One evening in 1982, five people were pulled from their home in a rural settlement near Estación Cocorná and assassinated by armed paramilitary men in what would turn out to be one of the more notable massacres in the history of the village. The paramilitaries, a group called Autodefensas de Puerto Boyacá (Self-Defenders of Puerto Boyacá), hailed from an important nearby Magdalena port town and notorious paramilitary breeding ground that I would pass through on my way out of Estación Cocorná.

The slain were followers of a prominent priest in Estación Cocorná, Bernardo López Arroyave, whose community programs brought rumors of a Marxist revolutionary insurrection. In this case, López Arroyave was said to be a supporter of the ELN—the National Liberation Army, the major guerrilla group that dominated the Magdalena Medio and held the distinction of being the second-largest guerrilla force in all of Colombia after the FARC—and the paramilitaries planned to assassinate him at a wedding he was set to officiate in town. Receiving word of the planned attempt on his life, López Arroyave fled on the train north to Barrancabermeja the morning of the wedding. That evening, armed men showed up at the home of the Buitrago family, some of the priest's closest devotees, and found two brothers, their cousin, their uncle, and a friend just returned from playing in a soccer game. They took the five of them out of the house and shot them. The youngest was just ten years old.

The massacre jolted the community. The surviving Buitrago family members also fled to Barrancabermeja, joining the ever-growing number of Colombians forcibly displaced by local violence. Others who remained in Estación Cocorná joined the ELN. They named their battalions Bernardo López Arroyave, after their leader, and Carlos Alirio Buitrago, after the two brothers, Carlos and Alirio, who were killed in the massacre that drove the people to enlist.

I would later go on to meet a former ELN guerrilla soldier one afternoon on Isabel's patio. His name was Guillermo Rodríguez, but everyone called him Patolandia. He joined the ELN in the 1970s, aged just fourteen, he told me, because he hoped for a revolution for the life of the forgotten campesinos—the farmers, shepherds, and fishermen of Colombia's more rural regions. After a year of fighting, he was jailed by the government for two years, during which time he became disillusioned with the guerrilla movement. "Bombing bridges, kidnapping people, that's not a revolution," he told me. "That's wrong." As soon as he was released, he returned to Estación Cocorná, where he has worked as a lime gatherer ever since. (For more recent ex-combatants—mostly FARC guerrillas demobilized in the past few years—the societal reintegration process has been difficult and wrought with stigma. Not unlike Colombia's social and environmental leaders, hundreds of ex-combatants committed to re-incorporation have been murdered by paramilitaries and other dissident criminal groups since the 2016 peace agreement was signed.)

But that late afternoon, shielded from the low, hazy sun that baked the empty town streets, eighty-eight-year-old Aurelio recalled to me a particular incident that would forever remain burned into his memory. "One Sunday, two people were killed in broad daylight." He pointed to the plaza, where four schoolchildren were now quietly playing basketball. "Pa! Pa!" He imitated the sound of gunshots. "I remember it. Right there." Such occurrences were common decades ago, he said, and in recent years things had calmed down. He preferred to remember the better times, when the river was rich and so was the town, when he would spend his days on river beaches collecting turtle eggs to sell in Puerto Boyacá—something he now thinks of as unfathomable, because of Isabel's river turtle sanctuary and the fact that the community is behind the conservation of eggs and the release of baby turtles back into the wild. "She's going to kill me for saying this," he said of Isabel, laughing, "but I ate thousands of turtles back then."

For some reason, before we parted ways, it occurred to me to ask

Aurelio, a man who'd lived his whole life in the landlocked Magdalena Medio, if he'd ever been to the sea. He saw the ocean once, he said, in Santa Marta with Isabel, and that was enough for him. "The sea is too scary," he added, shaking his head. "And dangerous."

———

IF AURELIO COULD BE COUNTED AMONG ESTACIÓN CO-corná's oldest residents, a boy named Gregory and his family were some of its newest. When I met Gregory at Isabel's house, the skinny twelve-year-old had been living in town for less than a year. He came to Colombia with his family—his mother, Milena; his stepfather, José Israel; his older brother, Yoel; and his younger half sister, Jazmín—after spending most of his life in a small town in the seasonally flooded plains of western Venezuela. They found their way to Estación Cocorná by way of José Israel, whose relatives had already settled in the village and were working as farmhands on nearby land. José Israel was working as a repairman along the motobalinera track, which earned him a salary of roughly $250 per month. For them, the relative calm of Estación Cocorná was a better option than Venezuela, where massive inflation and the rule of the despotic strongman Nicolas Maduro has led to catastrophic poverty, hunger, and violence. Since 2014, more than 5 million Venezuelans have fled what has become Latin America's worst humanitarian crisis.

That summer, news of incoming Venezuelan refugees was sweeping the nation, and all along the Magdalena I found traces of them. I watched as cattle trucks arrived in small riverside towns, unloading migrants instead of livestock under the cover of night. On television, cameras documented forlorn, tired families that had just crossed the border on foot, lugging sacks filled with what little they could carry. The papers published the statistics: roughly nine hundred thousand Venezuelans were thought to be living in Colombia while I was in Estación Cocorná, in mid-2018, with an estimated fifty thousand more arriving each month. That figure has since risen to a total of nearly 2 million people.

Just as Venezuela had accepted Colombians during the height of displacement caused by the armed conflict, Colombia was letting the migrants through, almost without question. Most Colombians I spoke with at the time supported this, recalling the terrors of their own past, and in early 2021, the Colombian government announced a landmark plan to grant the migrants temporary legal status. But the plan is not without opponents. Xenophobic rhetoric blaming Venezuelans for increases in crime is becoming more common—though research suggests that the refugees are more likely to be victims than perpetrators of crime themselves. A handful of people I met while making my way along the Magdalena in 2018 were already angry about the potential economic implications of their government's willingness to absorb the newcomers. "Back in Venezuela, many worked as doctors, bank managers—honorable jobs," one Colombian woman told me on a bus in the Huila Department, not far from the Magdalena's source. Most Venezuelan refugees in Colombian cities and towns have turned to informal work, barely scraping by, and many live in camps and on the streets. But with few other formal opportunities in the countryside besides working manual-labor jobs on farms, the woman feared, the migrants would soon threaten the job security of people like her husband.

Indeed, in Estación Cocorná, jobs were already scarce—while José Israel was able to find work on the railroad track, his brother, a more recent arrival, could only find a job on a farm that was miles away, returning to his home in the village to see his wife and daughter once every two or three weeks. José Israel's younger sister—just seventeen years old when I met her—had not attended school since walking here from Venezuela with her one-year-old daughter. In Estación Cocorná, she worked sporadically for the sediment harvesters on the Magdalena and lamented the fact that there was hardly any steady work to find in town. She spent most days in the arms of a man six years her senior, and I wondered where the child's father was. Months after I left, the two started dating, and I heard that she'd stopped working altogether.

It was a weekend afternoon in town when I met Gregory for the first time. I was sitting at the river's edge with Alvarito, Daniel, and some of the kids—most of them Venezuelan—listening to music out of their large black loudspeaker. Alvarito was playing all of his favorite English songs for me so I could translate the lyrics into Spanish to the group's delight. But he only knew a few, which meant that I was on my third translation of Oasis's "Wonderwall" when Gregory tapped me on the shoulder.

"Hi. Do you want to go fishing with me?" he asked shyly, looking up at me with a toothy grin. I recognized him—his slightly crossed eyes, fair skin, and freckles set him apart from most of the other children who played around Isabel's house—but I did not remember his name. Yet, never one to turn down a potential fishing opportunity, I jumped from my seat.

"Hey, boludo!" A few days earlier, I'd taught Alvarito an endearing Argentine nickname, which he promptly began using every time he saw me, his "Argentine friend." This time, he felt slighted. "We're in the middle of a song!"

I smiled. "It's too bad you don't have a guitar here," I joked as Gregory ran excitedly to get his fishing supplies. "Otherwise, I'd sing it for you."

After a few minutes, Gregory returned with a coil of fishing line wrapped around an old plastic bottle, along with a bag filled with a mushy orange substance. "This is fishing dough," he said very matter-of-factly and gave me the bag to hold. I opened it and pulled off a piece of the dough, which was mealy and broke apart easily, leaving an orange Cheetos-like stain on my fingers that smelled vaguely of chili.

I followed Gregory to four canoes that were docked in the slow-moving water, each one tied to the next, with the largest secured to a tree on the shore by a long rope. The noontime sun had baked the boats, and our feet were burning by the time we climbed to the one farthest from the shore. We sat on the starboard side of the canoe, our legs hanging over the edge in the cool, muddy water that had been stirred up by the previous night's rains. Gregory took a piece of dough to bait the hook and then tossed it into the river, just a few feet from the boat. He sat and held the line tensely. I watched as the line began to twitch immediately upon entering the water. "Nibbles," Gregory said. If he felt a bite, he yanked the line hard—so hard that the hook would soar out of the water—before pulling it back into the boat. He came up empty on the first several attempts, the dough needing replacement after having been dissolved or pecked away. Finally, after around fifteen minutes, a fish leapt out of the water when Gregory pulled the line, and the hook was set in its mouth—it couldn't have been more than six inches long, but any fish was better than no fish. *Leporinus muyscorum*, Isabel later told me, a species endemic to Colombia and identified by three large black spots along its sides. Gregory brought the fish in and laid it down on the hot floor of the boat, where it panicked for a few seconds before dying without much of a fight.

We caught three more in that way. Gregory let me try once he was certain he wouldn't go home to his parents empty-handed. It took me a few bites before I was able to pull quickly enough to set the hook. My own small catch, of the same species, came flying out of the water. At one point, Gregory's seven-year-old cousin Marley joined us and caught a fish on her first cast. After more than an hour, our skin scorched and stained orange, we waded to shore victorious, with the five oily fish in our hands. Gregory promptly gutted and scaled them whole before bringing them home. He was happy, because they would be his family's deep-fried dinner that night.

When we got back to Isabel's, Alvarito and the rest of the group were grinning at me—presumably, I thought, because they were gleefully awaiting another round of musical translations. I was wrong. Alvarito pulled out an acoustic guitar.

"Vaaaaamos, boludo!" he said, holding it out toward me.

I couldn't believe it. "Do any of you know how to play?" They shook their heads.

"Not a fucking clue." Alvarito laughed. "We got it from the priest."

"What should we sing?" I asked, taking the guitar from him.

"'Wonderwall!'" Alvarito chose without hesitating. It was the only song everyone knew. "Sing to her." He pointed me toward Mayra, a young Venezuelan woman not much older than me, who was sitting in one of the chairs. She shot me a flirtatious smile. Every day, Alvarito tried to set me up with a different girl. Nothing seemed to hold him back (earlier, I'd met Mayra's husband).

"Nope, that's not happening." I turned back to Alvarito. "We can sing this one together."

"Okay, okay." Alvarito was excited, despite knowing full well that constantly listening to the song on repeat did not mean he knew a single word of the lyrics. But with that, I began to strum and sing.

By then, a crowd of more children and onlookers gathered. Gregory stood beside me, while Alvarito mumbled some words in an attempt to sing along. Many of the adults were recording the "performance" on their cell phones.

I didn't know what it was about this song, of all the English songs they knew, that resonated with them so much. I sang it awkwardly, for the guitar was spectacularly out of tune and trying to adjust the strings didn't do much good in the extreme humidity. Yet the people of Estación Cocorná pretended not to notice, I think out of respect, as they stood around with wide smiles on their faces. Indeed, while few generalizations can be made about an entire country, it was clear everywhere I went that Colombians are tremendously respectful people.

Alvarito showed the grainy video of me singing that song to everyone we met after that, his way of introducing me. "My great friend, el boludo Jord!" he would say, still not completely sure how to fully pronounce my name. He always played the audio through his loudspeaker, cranking up the volume for the whole town to hear. Even a few days later, when Alvarito, Daniel, Gregory, and Gregory's brother, Yoel, took me by boat to the bus station in Puerto Boyacá, the nearest big town along the Magdalena, Alvarito found friends who owned a bar and made them play it too. I cringed as the booming Colombian rap was silenced in favor of the fuzzy audio of an out-of-tune guitar and my poor singing voice. Alvarito and the others grinned at me as they enjoyed icy Coca-Colas.

It was interesting to see the four of them in this context, removed from the quiet of Estación Cocorná, in what was basically a small city. Just a few hours earlier, we'd all stripped down to our boxers to wade a mile up the knee-high Magdalena, pulling our boat toward deeper water—it couldn't motor any farther because the river was too low. The morning was quiet; the riverbed felt clean, not muddy but composed of small, smooth stones that massaged our bare feet, and the water felt warm and silky. At one point, Alvarito thought he brushed a stingray with his toes.

In Puerto Boyacá, the chaotic streets were crowded with fruit-juice vendors, share-taxis, motorcycles, cargo trucks piled high with straw sacks of food, donkeys pulling carts, humans pulling carts—a far cry from the quiet village roads of dirt and dust. It reminded me of Girardot. Daniel relished the chance to walk past air-conditioned clothing stores, sighing with relief every time the doors opened and frigid air blew onto his face. Before they left me at the bus station, I invited them to a restaurant of Alvarito's choice for a lunch of grilled meat served with rice, beans, and a bowl of lentil soup. I quickly realized that it was the most substantial meal that Gregory and Yoel had eaten in weeks. The Venezuelan brothers cleaned their plates completely, leaning back in their seats when they were finished, hands on their stomachs, fully satisfied.

AT TIMES, ESTACIÓN COCORNÁ WAS SO TRANQUIL THAT IT was easy to forget its difficult past, or even its troubled present. Early one morning, a group of about a dozen soldiers carrying machine guns silently trundled by us on the river beach. We took note immediately, sitting up just a tad straighter in our plastic chairs and speaking in quieter, hushed tones. I say "we" because I, too, was on edge—and of that, the soldiers took note in return. I sensed their side-eyed glances as they milled about; I did not belong. I waited, certain that one of them would approach me. No one did. "These are their normal rounds," Alvarito said, trying to reassure me. They had spent the night. Estación Cocorná was so safe, he suggested, that it didn't even have police.

The first time I'd had a run-in with the Colombian military was on a bus crossing into the Huila Department, en route to San Agustín and Quinchana, near the Magdalena's source. Men in green camo waved the bus down to the side of the road. I turned to two girls who had just sat down next to me, and quietly asked them what was going on.

"It's nothing to worry about," one of the girls said. They giggled.

One soldier boarded and ordered all of the men and their bags off the bus. Women could stay, they announced. I rose from my seat, uneasy, and smacked my head on the overhead luggage shelf. The girls giggled once more.

"Are you sure I have nothing to worry about?" I whispered.

They did not look up from their smartphones, which they were using to exchange emoji-filled text messages of heart-eyed faces in giant font. Such an event was clearly not troubling them as much as it was troubling me.

The rest of the soldiers were waiting for us as we got off the bus. They began going through bags and patting down some of the men. To everyone except me, this seemed to be a formality, and they were going through the motions without a second thought: hands on the bus, arms outstretched until you were examined more thoroughly than at the airport. The soldiers hardly spoke and looked extremely unhappy in their present positions. I noticed their black leather boots with laces, relieved not to be seeing the distinctive black rubber galoshes of the guerrillas. Only a few years earlier, I'd been told, this Tolima–Huila highway was a hot spot for insurgent checkpoints, where passengers could be robbed or abducted. It was still considered a risky road to travel at night. After searching a few of the passengers, and before they reached me, the soldiers told us we could reboard the bus and continue on our way.

Back in Estación Cocorná, later in the day, the town loudspeaker crackled to life. A man's muffled voice announced an important meeting that would be taking place at 4:00 p.m. on the plaza in the center of town. The army would be in attendance. Nobody stopped to listen to the announcement, and as far as I knew, not many people ultimately attended the meeting, which was in preparation for an anticorruption referendum vote that would take place the next day.

Just two years earlier, I had been in Colombia on the eve of another, more significant referendum vote: the referendum on peace. It was August of 2016, and I was in a village called Cotocá Arriba, not unlike Estación Cocorná, along the banks of the Sinú River in the northern department of Córdoba. (That town, too, had a community-based river turtle conservation project—and in fact, the leader of that initiative, a young, enterprising man named Luis

Carlos Negrette, was the first person to put me in touch with Isabel in Estación Cocorná.) As in Estación Cocorná, it seemed as though talk of the referendum (even such a serious one) did not proliferate in Cotocá Arriba, a quiet village set among a vast depression of rural wetlands that had for many years been plagued by paramilitaries and guerrillas both. Perhaps it was my presence that made such topics off-limits for discussion; while I was there, people seemed interested only in telling me about Colombia's newfound safety and growing potential for foreign tourism. One older man was planning to slaughter a pig at the end of the week, which apparently required great preparation. All this to say, there were things that just seemed to take priority.

That afternoon in Estación Cocorná, instead of discussing politics and participating in the gathering, the group was getting ready to fly kites. There were only so many days left in August, the month when a dry wind swept over the land and Colombians across the country filled the sky with dancing colors. To not fly would be a waste of an entire day. I stumbled upon their preparations on the road in front of Isabel's yellow house. Alvarito, always the village's handyman, was also its kite master—working with thin bamboo sticks, pieces of tissue paper, and colorful plastic bags, he built dozens of kites each year, swarmed by a crowd of eager children. There was a clear hierarchy with regard to who could do what. Alvarito, Daniel, and Diego, Alvarito's twenty-two-year-old stepson, were the leaders, directing the older children in gluing, tying knots, and preparing the more ambitious kites for the day's flight. Indeed, the older children, who were mostly teenagers, were the most impatient to get in on the action; the others, as young as four years old, were too timid to do anything but look on and admire the process. Everyone was always discussing—debating the structural integrity of their existing kites and attempting to build more from new designs. Alvarito showed me the best kind of string, tough and sharp, attached to the kite itself by the clip of a steel fishing leader. That string was reserved for the most complex kite: a large, three-foot pyramid composed of ten smaller tissue-paper pyramids within it, colored yellow, red, green, and blue. It was large and heavy, and along the reaches of the Magdalena, where the hot, stubborn air sinks in the valley and the wind rarely blows, it was hard to imagine that any breeze at all would be strong enough to lift it off the ground.

"I don't mean to interrupt," I said to Alvarito, hovering over his shoulder beside three children while he tied a knot to the steel leader, "but there isn't any wind. How are you going to be able to fly these with no wind?"

"We're going to a special spot with more wind, so the kites get picked up." Alvarito smiled, keeping his eyes fixed on the wire. Beads of sweat dripped down his thick neck from the inner band of his wide-brimmed hat—a sombrero vueltiao, the signature cowboy hat of Colombia, made from intricately woven stalks of grass—onto his dark-brown T-shirt, dyed on the back with thin beige letters reading ALVARITO.

"And where is that?" I asked.

"Pa'alla!" he answered, still concentrating while flicking his head in a vague direction.

"How are we going to get there?"

"We'll go on the motos, and the kids will run to catch up on foot." The hierarchy at work again—I had somehow made it to the top.

Soon enough, when the final adjustments were made, Daniel, Diego, Alvarito, and I doubled up on the motorcycles and zoomed off.

While Alvarito drove, I was in charge of his favorite kite: a long, flat pentagon colored red, white, and green. Though I held tightly on to the intersection of the frame, it was still a challenge to keep it steady as we blew through the air, the motorcycle maneuvering wildly through the streets of the village. We followed the train tracks for a while, eventually crossing them before winding up some small hills just to the east. As the ground rose, we passed a wireless signal tower and a small maintenance hut. Only around five minutes after setting off, a freestanding grassy mound appeared just off-road. We parked the motos and squeezed through a barbed-wire cattle fence to reach the base of the mound, scrambling up its side on all fours. Around us, the hilly pastures and wetlands of the Magdalena Medio stretched out toward the horizon; to the west, the flatlands reached to the mountains of Antioquia, the Central Cordillera, and to the east I could make out the jagged peaks of the eastern range of the Andes. The light was growing long in the valley, and a full moon was visible above us. Then, atop the grassy mound, suddenly I felt it: a strong, steady wind picked up from the north, rippling our shirts and causing the stalks of grass to sway back and forth.

Alvarito wasted no time in releasing his kite, the one I'd been holding on to. His string was wrapped tightly around an old plastic bottle and tied at the neck, just below the cap. All he had to do was turn the bottle and release more string for the breeze to easily lift the kite into the sky.

"One hundred meters of string," Alvarito said, nodding toward his creation, now just a blip floating high in the air, grounded only by a single white arching filament that led back to his hands. Against all odds, the heavy pyramid made it up, too. The rays of the sun passed through the translucent tissue paper, making the kites shimmer as they danced, rising and falling with the wind, like specks on a wave in a faraway sea. Someone on a hillside several miles away was flying a kite of his own, and Alvarito took note.

"Hey!" Alvarito yelled over the snapping of plastic in the wind.

"Hey!" came the faint response, rising up through the still air of the valley below, followed by something unintelligible.

"He said he's pulling his in, heading home for the night," said Alvarito, deciphering for those of us who could not hear. Sure enough, the faraway kite soon started descending back toward the land. "Not us!" Alvarito laughed proudly.

Suddenly, there were squeals of excitement—some of the kids had arrived, out of breath from having run up the same winding roads we'd climbed on the motos out of town, past the cemetery and through the hills, despite the suffocating heat and humidity. Many of them held their own small kites. Gregory carried a purple kite hitched to the same bottle-and-string apparatus he used to go fishing—another reminder that, as with most of what went on in Estación Cocorná, even the kites were tied to the river. "Look at the caña brava," Alvarito had said to me when we were on the Magdalena, pointing out the tall shoots of wild grass that grew along the riverbank and came floating downstream with the current. "The stalks can be used for many different things," he said, "but I use them to make kites." All sorts of flotsam from the rivers could be used to create kites, in fact, from caña brava for the frame to colorful plastic bags for the flaps and tail. That's half of the effort—making the most from what you have.

7

No Name

A SIGN BESIDE A TURNOFF ON THE ROAD NORTH POINTED toward the town of Puerto Berrío. I didn't go. There, two hours downriver from where the hippopotamuses of the Magdalena wallow in the shallows, people go to the cemetery to visit the tombs of people they have never met.

The corpses lie in a long, cement structure of rectangular slots stacked one upon another like colorful PO boxes. They had arrived, like many living people used to in Puerto Berrío seventy or eighty years ago, by river: killed somewhere in conflict upstream, they were discarded in death, dumped into the Magdalena and carried away by the current. Their families, meanwhile, were left searching for answers.

It's not that many of them weren't noticed before reaching Puerto Berrío. As recently as a decade ago, when thousands of deaths were brought about by war, it was normal for fishermen in the villages of the Magdalena Medio to encounter corpses several times a day, facedown in the water as they floated past, caught in swirling eddies or snagged on submerged trees. So frequent were these sightings, in fact, that many onlookers ignored cadavers like they would a log or a branch—or worse, they would unsnag them from their obstacles before leaving them to continue their slow journeys downriver. Ferry drivers and other motorboaters sped past them, too, leaving lifeless bodies spinning and bobbing in the chaos of their wakes. Some corpses would make it all the way to the Caribbean, however many hundreds of towns and miles and onlookers that meant passing in the process, to be ignored one last time by a coastal fisherman or freighter, perhaps, before disappearing for good into the sea.

But of the ones who didn't make it to the sea—those who were noticed and pulled in elsewhere along the way—many were brought ashore in Puerto Berrío, a town that has long suffered from its own share of conflict-related violence. During the days of steamboat transportation, Puerto Berrío was an important example of Colombia's potential for a modern, multimodal economy. Steamboats running to and from the coast dropped off passengers there for westbound trains to Medellín, back when the service was still maintained, and replenished their own storerooms with bulging loads of coffee beans and sugarcane. Other railroad lines, like the one that passed through Estación Cocorná, connected Berrío with points north and south. It was a strategic port, a crossroads for trade and transport, a place where the people of the mountains came down to the riverbanks and sold their wares.

The same "Death to Kidnappers" militia that marked the early days of the paramilitaries devastated Puerto Berrío from the moment the group was established in the 1980s, massacring farmers, murdering schoolteachers, and instilling a reign of terror over the land. The contraband-plagued river port hadn't much recovered since: even when I was making my own way downriver, during a time of relatively unprecedented mobility and peace in the Magdalena Medio, I was only given a handful of names and phone numbers and told to call instead—no one agreed to help me get there.

But cadavers do not have much of a choice in these matters, and in Puerto Berrío more than thirty years ago the fishermen started bringing them in whenever they came across them on the river. They called each corpse N.N., for "ningún nombre"—no name. One by one, the town cemetery began accumulating them: N.N. 1, N.N. 2, N.N. 3 . . . After all, the town had plenty of its own "disappeared" from the war, and if anything, giving a final resting place to others' missing loved ones was a sort of consolation for those who'd lost their own. Perhaps it meant that somewhere, someone else would do the same for them.

Between eighty thousand and one hundred thousand people are thought to have disappeared in Colombia from 1958 to 2018 due to conflict, according to varying estimates. Around a thousand of them are buried in Puerto Berrío—hardly a dent in the national figure but likely more than in any other known single town in Colombia. What sets Berrío apart is the dedication its residents have shown to the N.N.s—families took to adopting them, *naming* them (sometimes after their own disappeared loved ones), caring for their tombs as they would for those of close relatives—in the hopes that they would bring good luck.

"Each N.N. is treated as if it were a saint," a fisherman named Edgar Iván Maldonado told me on the phone from Berrío. He'd been bringing in N.N.s since the beginning: "People paint the tombs, name the cadavers, ask them for things." Some have credited their N.N.s with bringing them successful relationships, wealthy lovers, and even lottery windfalls.

These days, people told me all along the river, the flow of corpses down the Magdalena has slowed. And in Puerto Berrío, residents said the numbing of normalcy of war is beginning to wear off—to see one, blue and bloated in the choppy waters of the river, is more startling and surprising than in years past. But it also means that Berrío has seen fewer and fewer of them arriving at its shores—a bad omen for those families still hoping for an adopted N.N. of their own. Rumors coming out of the town say that, so as not to cause battles among the townspeople, any rare new arrivals are now buried away from the main group of N.N.s, hidden from the eager miracle seekers in unmarked graves. Just like in the rest of the country, forgotten once more.

8

Hostage of the Magdalena

I STAYED ON THE BUS BOUND FOR ONE OF COLOMBIA'S smallest major cities, which also happened to be among its richest. Barrancabermeja, not a tourist destination or a source of national pride by many standards, was home to the few chalupas (small, fast ferries) that still ran the remaining navigable course of the Magdalena. Mine was to depart at dawn in two days' time, a six-hour downstream bullet that would leave me not far from the legendary town of Mompox.

For all that it is not, Barrancabermeja, with a population smaller than that of many U.S. suburbs, has trudged on through the past half century of decline as arguably the most important city along the course of the Magdalena, at least in economic terms. The rusting smokestacks that loom over the city quickly reveal why: oil rules this river town, and as the winds change direction every afternoon, the stench of a thousand gaslights wafts into the corners of every home and business in the area.

Understandably, it is looked upon by outsiders as not much more than a gritty oil port, its sandbanks muddied and grayed by the contamination from its refineries. Yet, despite its unsympathetic reputation, I found parts of Barrancabermeja to be quite charming for the commercial and industrial town that it was. Every few blocks yielded a three-story, open-air shopping mall, in which all of the stalls sold either knockoff cell phone accessories or ad-plastered imitation soccer jerseys hailing from every country of Latin America. In some neighborhoods, the layout of the gridded streets and tree-lined boulevards almost felt like the United States. Indeed, such a comparison wasn't too far off: before state-owned Ecopetrol—the largest oil company in the country—took over in 1961, you could have mistaken Barrancabermeja for a Texas oil town. Subsidiaries of Standard Oil Company and ExxonMobil were the first to build up the industry in the 1920s, single-handedly turning the sleepy Magdalena fishing village into a metropolis of nearly two hundred thousand people. American oilmen flooded the town, arriving on the luxurious Magdalena riverboats from the Caribbean coast, and private schools were founded to serve their families. Though most of the Americans had long gone, some of their schools, now bilingual, still remained.

I'd reserved a room at the Radisson, one of a handful of new hotels that had opened in Barrancabermeja in recent years. It was modern, with thick glass windows and more than a dozen stories; on the rooftop terrace, there was a chic bar and restaurant with cushioned wicker chairs. The young, opinionated taxi driver seemed disappointed in me when we arrived.

"If you're interested in the Magdalena," he said, "you should have stayed at the Hotel Pipatón." He shook his head. "It's closing for good in a day or two. The gem of Barranca, and of the Río Magdalena."

I thought for a moment. *Hotel Pipatón.* I'd never heard of the place, but then again, my knowledge of Barrancabermeja was limited—while it was one of the most important points along the river in economic terms, the only reason I was there was to find onward river transportation, and it had appeared that there was not otherwise very much for a visitor to see. The sun was setting. I quickly thanked the driver and stepped out of the car into the heat of the night. My chalupa north was not scheduled to leave for another thirty-six hours, and I was looking for a way to spend my spare day in the city. Perhaps the Hotel Pipatón was it.

———

I'LL ADMIT, I DID NOT EXPECT THE CLOSING OF ONE OF Colombia's grandest hotels to involve a water-aerobics class for senior citizens. It was a Monday afternoon, about four o'clock. The winds had just shifted direction, and the hot fumes of the oil refineries drifted through the sweeping archways and open-air corridors of the majestic Hotel Pipatón into its center courtyard with antique metal chairs and wide green umbrellas overlooking a sparkling-blue rectangular pool. The old ladies, bobbing about on foam noodles, didn't seem to mind the smell, while those of us without bathing suits and swim caps (mainly their elderly husbands, and me) were left envying their position in the cool water. A handful of workers who comprised the remaining skeleton staff of the hotel milled about completing their final chores, sweeping the patio and tending to the empty poolside bar.

Oscar Castilla, the hotel's general manager, occasionally stepped out of his air-conditioned back office to peruse what was left of the hotel's activity. He was a short, dark-skinned man in his sixties, with shiny gray hair slicked back. When I first met Oscar, I spoke with him in Spanish for several minutes before he told me he'd lived in the United States for nearly thirty years.

"Come on, man," I said with a smile, switching to English. "This must have been fun for you."

"I was a Vietnam vet," Oscar replied, grinning, over the blare of a large metal fan. "I got my degree at City College of New York!"

Then why in the world did you come to Barrancabermeja? I thought, and before the words could escape my lips, Oscar asked the same of me. It's not that I hadn't gotten used to these kinds of questions before. I first fielded them on my original trip to Colombia, as I lay in the hammocks with Colo and Vismar in Ladrilleros; the questions continued in San Agustín, in Estación Cocorná, and now in Barrancabermeja. Questions about why I'd come inevitably brought follow-ups about who I was, and these answers were less clear. Was I Argentine? My accent revealed it, but something was off. Where was I from? New York—that made more sense. And my last name, what was it? Arabic, Middle Eastern, okay, there were people with that name in Colombia, too. But what was my religion? Though my answer to this question was certain, it was often the trickiest one, for every Jew knows we are sometimes unwelcome.

I often take to thinking about how I came to be such an ethnic and cultural mixed bag. My mother's ancestors thrived among the once wealthy and prominent Jewish community in Baghdad, but she and her family fled a world of religious persecution, of baseless hangings and jailings, and came to New York in the 1970s with very little. My paternal great-grandparents—working-class Jews from Damascus and Aleppo facing forced non-Muslim military conscription by the Ottomans in the early 1900s—escaped by ship to Buenos Aires, where my grandparents grew up poor, sometimes even hungry. My grandfather, the first in his family to attend a university, received his MD in Argentina; he married my grandmother, and they moved to Brooklyn. And my parents met, by some stroke of fate, in the cafeteria line during their own first week of medical school in Manhattan.

As the children of a Syrian Argentine father and an Iraqi mother in the New York suburbs, my brothers and I grew up around Spanish, Arabic, and Hebrew. But because my parents' single common tongue was English, that was the language of our house. Only once I started studying it in middle school did the broken pieces of my spoken Spanish finally come together.

Perhaps the most American thing about me is that at home in the United States, where I was born and have lived my entire life, I've always felt slightly out of place. So, strange as it is, I've found that the more I travel to communities themselves out of the way and misunderstood, the more I'm forced to explain myself, over and over again, to different kinds of people I meet—and the better sense I'm able to make of my own identity once I'm back home. That, perhaps, was one of the main reasons I was drawn in by Colombia, the Magdalena, and places like Barrancabermeja.

I did not say these things to Oscar; probably I mumbled something about my interest in the way things used to be. A long time ago

Barrancabermeja, and the Hotel Pipatón, were not out of the way at all: finished in 1943, the Pipatón was the hotel of choice for passengers heading to and from Bogotá, the logistical halfway point between the capital and the coast. Even as it stopped receiving a steady influx of guests from the boats, it kept its reputation as the gathering place for any well-to-do visitors in town. The upper echelons of Barrancabermeja society came to swim in the Pipatón's large pool and eat in its air-conditioned restaurant, with its red tablecloths and sweeping views of the river.

I got on well enough with Oscar for him to invite me to lunch—or, perhaps, just three days away from shuttering the hotel's doors, he didn't have anything better to do. He told me the story of his own life as it related to the story of the hotel he took care of for so many years. At noon that Monday, the restaurant was filled to capacity, mainly by large groups of older couples enjoying the day's fixed menu of steak, rice, and colorful salads, bookended by chicken soup and creamy sundae desserts. In fact, if you didn't realize that almost all of the rooms in the place were empty—save for one history enthusiast who, according to Oscar, fell in love with the building and wanted to ride out its final days as its final guest—the hotel gave no overt indication of its impending closure. On the main floor, the grand ballroom was the only glaringly empty space, the numerous ceiling fans motionless above its barren red-tiled dance floor. Its arching doors, their wooden frames now decaying, used to be made of glass imported from Milan.

"Now," Oscar said, rapping loudly on them to yield the sound of pure plastic, "it's all cheap Plexiglas."

———

THE STORY OF THE HOTEL BEGINS IN THE SIXTEENTH century, with its namesake: the cacique Pipatón, leader of the Yariguí tribe that once lived on the very land where the hotel now sits, in the dense forests on the eastern bank of the river.

It was 1536 when the Spanish conquistador Gonzalo Jiménez de Quesada and his men happened upon the Yariguíes, during their expedition up the Magdalena (then called the river Yuma by Indigenous peoples—paradoxically, the "river of friends"), because the waters of the great river were so swollen with rain that it was too treacherous to proceed any farther. "The river was so high that it overflowed its own shores, flooding the lands and the fields, making it impossible to even walk along its edge," Jiménez de Quesada observed.

The conquistador instructed his men to set up inland camp to pass the remaining months of the wet season, and in the months and years that followed, the Spanish proceeded to wage several vicious attacks on the Yariguíes. Pipatón, who governed with his wife Yarima, put up a famously strong fight, evading several attempts at capture, but was ultimately defeated—his heels sliced off, according to some stories—and exiled. The few Yariguí people who survived after decades of fighting were decimated by disease transmitted to them by their colonizers in the centuries that followed. It was a slow, cruel, generations-long demise. Only in the twentieth century, after oil speculators logged and mined their way onto the already stolen Yariguí land, was the tribe declared extinct.

The Spanish called the area Barrancabermeja—"barranca" meaning "gully" and "bermeja" meaning "russet-colored"—to describe the reddish-brown riverbanks that were characteristic of this part of the Magdalena Medio. In 1936, precisely four hundred years after the landing of Jiménez de Quesada, construction began on the planned Hotel Nacional de Barrancabermeja, which would ultimately bear the name of the conquistador's most formidable rival, Pipatón.

The hotel sat on prime real estate, on a bend in the river that forms the southern edge of the city, far enough from the oil refineries that only the tips of the gas flares were visible in the distance. This was the small "old town" of Barrancabermeja, and it was hard to imagine that it could ever have resembled the colonial pastels and cobblestones of Cartagena or San Juan or Havana. But there, just up the block, was the site of the first church, a simple straw hut built in 1601; on another corner across the street, the building with the first telegraph, and then the first telephone, that Barrancabermeja ever saw.

When the Magdalena thrived in its golden-age glory, so did the Hotel Pipatón. Night after night the ballroom was filled with music and dancing that would last until the crack of dawn, when the ship passengers dressed in white suits and gowns would retire to their rooms for a few hours' sleep in anticipation of what remained of their river journeys. Singers from all over the hemisphere came to perform, and the Pipatón soon rose to fame as the jewel of the hotel business in all of Colombia.

The story, by this point, is all too familiar. In the 1960s, steamboat travel declined, and so did life at the Hotel Pipatón. There were still guests every now and then—mainly those coming to do business with the oil companies that had set up permanent shop in the 1940s, in the process decimating the forests and the very last of the Yariguíes, who had survived the conquests by taking refuge in the remaining wilderness nearby. By the 1980s, the hotel was bankrupt, abandoned, and occupied by squatters. It made a comeback in the 1990s, financed by the local government, and in 1999 it was sold for three hundred thousand dollars to a private owner, who decided to hire his good friend Oscar Castilla for the position of general manager.

Oscar, who'd left Colombia for the United States in the early 1960s when his father took a job in Dayton, Ohio, jumped at the chance to move to Barrancabermeja and run the hotel. He'd already returned to the country of his birth seven years earlier, in 1992, owning and operating a fish farm on a plot of land on the Pacific coast just outside one of the country's most important maritime ports, the city of Buenaventura. He made good money—enough to pay the million-dollar ransom when he was kidnapped by the FARC and held captive for several days. And there was still money left over when he had to make good on his release clause, which consisted of extortion payments of several thousand dollars per month in order to avoid further kidnappings. He sent his wife and children to live elsewhere for their own safety and hired a bodyguard for himself—but until the 2016 peace deal was passed, he remained on the FARC "blacklist" for principal economic targets.

"I'm an adventurer," Oscar told me. "I move around. They say, 'Oscar, there's a new opportunity over there,' and I say, 'Which way?'"

Oscar's situation on the Pacific coast was perilous, to say the least, but life in Barrancabermeja in the early 2000s was not much easier. ELN guerrillas, who had ties with members of the Workers' Union of the Petroleum Industry (USO), controlled the industrial heart of the city for several years. By 1999, the United Self-Defense Forces of Colombia (AUC)—another of the most notorious paramilitary groups in the country—moved into the area to counter the

ELN's influence, setting up their headquarters in the outlying town of San Rafael de Lebrija.

"As a businessman in the city, I would be 'invited' to their check-in meetings," Oscar said of the AUC, very matter-of-factly. "You would pay the La Gómez toll, and then they'd monitor you until you got to the entrance to Lebrija, fifteen kilometers down the road. There, three or four men guarded the way into town with a clipboard, making sure everyone who was supposed to be at the meetings was accounted for."

The urban war for control over one of Colombia's most lucrative cities coincided with Oscar's arrival, and from the doorstep of the Hotel Pipatón, he observed it firsthand. "At first, there were only nine people on staff, so being the general manager meant doing it all," he said. "I was the night watchman, the gardener, everything. One night, I was standing guard out on the roundabout, right out there"—he turned to point out the window behind him, but the glare of the sun was too strong.

"Anyway, I noticed a suspicious-looking man walking up the road from the wharf district, coming this way. He stopped in the middle of the street, right across from the hotel. Looked like he was waiting for someone. Right then and there, I knew what was coming next.

"It was almost like it was timed, choreographed—another man coming now, pedaling on a bicycle, passing by the old church on his way downhill. When he rounded the corner, I heard six shots—bam! bam! bam! bam! bam! bam!—and threw myself to the ground." He shrugged. "When I got up, the cyclist was dead, and the assassin had gotten away."

Oscar recounted this as though he were reading me his tax returns. I was reminded of Jhon Alexander and the Quinchana villagers telling me stories about El Duende, of Aurelio Delgado Calderon and his memories of Estación Cocorná. There wasn't the slightest hint of fear in Oscar's voice.

"You would literally hear gunshots from all around the neighborhood," he said of his early days in Barrancabermeja. "Now, the fiber of the place has changed. You don't go to certain areas, of course, but it's a very dynamic city, very rich, moving millions of pesos. Money flows through this city. It's like none other in Colombia."

Indeed, money does flow through Barrancabermeja. That distinction, of course, has long been because of Ecopetrol. "Barranca is that," Oscar said, pointing to the refinery in the distance, "and nothing more." But the people at the city's helm, he said, have been mismanaging its funds for decades—of the city's previous four mayors, at the time, one was fending off several criminal charges, one was presently under house arrest, one had been sent to jail, and one was dead.

Yet oil always brought illusions of revival. Around 2010, Ecopetrol began negotiations on a major plan known as the Plan for Modernization of the Barrancabermeja Refinery (PMRB), which would upgrade its output capacity from 250,000 to 350,000 barrels of oil per day, adding up to fifteen thousand jobs. The ambitious plan, requiring more than three billion dollars in funding from the federal government, has proceeded in a stop-and-go manner since then. It was most recently postponed in 2016, with no renewed start date in sight.

The 2016 deferral sentenced the Hotel Pipatón to its death—not because the hotel itself did anything wrong but simply because there

were now too many others, many of them more modern than the Pipatón, that had been constructed in anticipation of the forthcoming
business. The demand, in the end, never came. Some of the unluck-
iest hotels finished construction just weeks before news of the 2016
PMRB decision broke. Mine, the Radisson, with its vacant rooms
and empty rooftop terrace, was one of them.

———

FOR MORE THAN A DECADE NOW THERE HAVE BEEN PLANS
to develop the entire Magdalena River basin, now often framed as
initiatives to revitalize Colombia's post-conflict economy and society.
Supporters of development envision massive barges easily cruising
between Barranquilla and La Dorada, each of them carrying seven
thousand tons of cargo—the equivalent of three hundred tractor
trailers' worth of freight. At certain key junctions like Puerto Berrío,
containers could be transferred between river, rail, and road. A new
shipping terminal opened in Barrancabermeja in 2016, and a freight
train has just recently returned to the rails along the river, terrifying
the motobalineras as it sporadically blasts through Estación Cocorná
on its way from Santa Marta to La Dorada. Many hope that the passenger trains will someday return, too.

The government-formed corporation that claims to be overseeing
all of these projects is called Cormagdalena (the Regional Autono-
mous Corporation for the Magdalena River), a painfully bureaucratic
and disorganized bunch. After many attempts at contacting them
with no response to show for it, I stumbled upon Cormagdalena's
headquarters in the wharf district of Barrancabermeja, just down the

road from the Hotel Pipatón. Its three-story building was flanked by wilting palm trees and stone-faced security guards and garnished with its logo: a water droplet painted in the red, blue, and yellow of the flag of Colombia. After I refused to accept the receptionist's assertion that every single person in the office was "extremely busy today," I was led upstairs to the desk of a rather perturbed engineer named Marlene.

"I'm not sure what you're exactly looking for here," Marlene said, shooting me side-eyed glances while typing away at her computer screen. This seemed to be the question of the day.

"I'm traveling along the length of the Magdalena, hoping to meet interesting people along its banks," I replied. "I'd like to know what Cormagdalena is doing to make the river navigable again."

Apparently, Marlene did not have an answer, or she was not authorized to give me the official one, because she responded by handing me several colorful coffee-table books that were recently made about the people of the Magdalena River, as well as, fittingly for the coffee-table books, a cup of sweet coffee to accompany my reading. I was content with flipping through the books and kept quiet for several minutes. Then, she gave me some contacts of local fishermen in the area, and we had a brief conversation about places I could visit around Barranca, though my chalupa would be leaving at dawn the next morning, and besides, I'd already spoken with plenty of fishermen who all gave pretty much the same testimony, which was significant: the river was getting drier, and the fish were getting smaller.

After about a half hour with Marlene, I realized that I wouldn't get very far sitting in the office of Cormagdalena, and later, based on several of their published documents, I realized that Cormagdalena wasn't getting very far in its objectives itself. Any realistic effort to restore navigability to the Magdalena would have to be monumental, and all of the initiatives that have already been planned have seen one setback after the next. Most dramatic was the tremendous fall from grace of the Brazilian construction giant Odebrecht, which, as part of the fallout of an international corruption scandal, saw a joint venture with its Colombian counterpart lose a $738 million contract to dredge and channelize the more than five hundred miles of river between Barranquilla and La Dorada. A bidding war for the rights erupted as a result, mainly between firms from China—ever expanding their influence throughout Latin America—and everyone else.

If the dredging work actually happens, environmentalists fear the worst: dried-up wetlands in some areas and tremendous flooding in others, the loss of spawning habitats in the riverbed, and a swifter, deeper river that would likely make any small-scale community-based transportation besides commercial barges treacherous. Add that to the already mounting troubles of global climate change—which, with intensifying droughts and more extreme weather events, has already begun wielding its earliest and most troubling effects on developing nations like Colombia—and the very riverside communities such projects are meant to revive will almost certainly be plunged deeper into despair.

It's not just the navigable Magdalena that is the aim of transformations that could forever alter its course. The ominously named Magdalena Master Plan—a four-hundred-page study drawn up by a Chinese private developer, the Chinese government, and Cormagdalena—extends to the farthest reaches of the Upper Magdalena, nearly as far as Quinchana. It calls for a network of hydropower projects to be built all over the rolling hills of the Colombian Massif. I caught a glimpse of two reservoirs, formed by dams that have existed for several years, out the window of a bus from San Agustín to Neiva. They looked like eerie floods among the mountains, and the surrounding landscape was, simply put, a lot less green: from what could be seen from the road, it wasn't a desert, but the grassy pastures had a bleaker, browner hue, and the farms (there were fewer, overall) had less of the characteristic deep, dark green of the highlands of the massif. The lakes sparkled under the rays of the setting sun; from afar, at least, there was no longer a sign of the brown, rushing river at all.

The big fear is that there will be more—eleven to fifteen dams are currently planned for the massif, in a country that already gets nearly 70 percent of its energy from hydropower, more than from any other source. "They say in the news that there will be more dams here, higher and higher in the mountains," one woman told me from beside her vegetable stand in the San Agustín market. "That would be disastrous." Environmentalists in the Huila Department have launched furious campaigns against the Master Plan, claiming dams would destroy local economies by consuming upstream farmlands with their floods and further decimating fish populations downstream with their interruption of the river's flow. Separate studies carried out in India, Norway, Spain, and China, among other countries, have supported the concerns of the environmentalists: hydropower, despite often being touted as a "green" source of energy, has destructive effects on the surrounding environment and riverside communities.

All along the length of the Magdalena there is already a great sense of loss and a desire to bounce back. But there is also the more overwhelming sense that there is still everything yet to lose.

———

FOR OSCAR CASTILLA, THE PIPATÓN WAS THE HOTEL THAT won his heart. He'd lived there, in the manager's quarters, until 2011— more than a decade—and spent years amassing a collection of thousands of photos and documents representing the hotel's history, which he spent thirty minutes downloading for me on two silver pen drives. It pained him to think of what would happen once the glorious Hotel Pipatón slipped out of his hands. While it would not be demolished— protected as a national historic landmark—the most likely of the options seemed to be a buyout from whichever organization was awarded long-term rights to dredge the Magdalena. The workers, who would spend week after week digging up the stones and the sludge of the riverbed, would sleep in the Pipatón's cozy suites; on their rest days, they would refresh themselves in its swimming pool.

"There's just so many stories, so much history." Oscar shook his head. "This was supposed to be our jubilee. Seventy-five years! But instead, we're closing down."

The Hotel Pipatón has forever been a hostage of the Río Grande de la Magdalena, to which all developments in Barrancabermeja seem inextricably tied. Over the course of three-quarters of a century, the Pipatón has risen and fallen with the river, a beneficiary of its days of grandeur and a victim of its days of despair. "We focused on the roads and the trucks, but we forgot that this is our main artery," Oscar said, looking out over the river. "This is our Mississippi."

9

Six Hours
by River

Port of Barrancabermeja, 6:00 a.m.

AT DAWN, PUSHING MY WAY THROUGH DOZENS OF PASSEN-
gers and boat hands to board the chalupa out of Barrancabermeja, I
realized how strange it was to be doing this now, and how normal it
would have been to have done it in the past.

The chaotic dock, small and hidden along the wharf zone, was
nothing more than a crumbling wooden platform shielded by a dark
metal roof; standing upon it, I quickly became dizzied by the sight of
the river, an ominous torrent rushing loudly beneath my feet, and it
felt as though, at any moment, the old dock could be swept away.

This moment, my only chance to legitimately use the Magdalena
to travel any significant distance from one place to another, had almost
slipped away from me. I'd been warned of the Cesar Department,

on the eastern bank of the river—wedged in between the Santander Department of Barrancabermeja and the Magdalena Department of El Banco, where I would disembark—one of the remaining hot spots of conflict, where paramilitaries and some guerrillas still wielded great influence. Over the course of what would be a six-hour journey by river, we would pass the San Lucas Mountains to the west—the real remaining no-man's-land of the Magdalena Medio—a heavily forested mountainous knot sprinkled with illegal gold mines and illicit coca plantations and ruled by ELN guerrillas. My university had implored me not to set foot in these places, suggesting that I travel accompanied along this stretch of river or not travel it at all. Add to that the notorious lack of maritime safety standards, and the number of fatal boat accidents in recent years, and there would be a very reasonable argument for traveling by bus instead.

But this was my only real chance to replicate part of the epic river journey that seemed so forever etched into the collective memory of Colombia, even if ever so slightly. Traveling by fast ferry, in the span of half a day I could now cover a distance that might have taken three or more by steamboat. Just beyond Barrancabermeja, I read over and over again, the river would widen tremendously. On either of its banks were the lands that, once thick with the trees of the jungle, so profoundly overwhelmed the likes of Simón Bolívar, "the Liberator," and the fictional Florentino Ariza from *Love in the Time of Cholera*. It remained one of the remotest parts of the entire river, a daunting stretch that was, in the words of García Márquez, "vast and solemn, like a swamp with no beginning or end," where "the heat was so dense you could touch it with your hands."

The chalupa was an oddly shaped vehicle, almost like a spaceship, completely covered, and slanted in the front but for a wide-open door in place of a windshield. I climbed through the front hatch to find thirty other passengers tightly packed into several rows of two-by-two seats. They all looked extremely tired and not nearly as excited as I was to be making the trip. Most of the passengers were middle-aged men and some elderly women. Two little girls in the front row clutched bright-pink backpacks. I was not sure who was accompanying them, as almost everyone else seemed to be traveling alone. One man shot me a piercing stare when I pulled out my camera to take a photograph. I took my place in the very last row, beside the window, where dozens of dead cockroaches littered the floor and the seat cushions. I flicked one off of my seat with my pinkie finger, and its leg twitched as it fell to the ground. I sat down.

"Let's take a selfie." My travel companion, Alejandra Mayorca, a nomadic woman with gentle eyes, pale skin, and dirty-blond hair, whipped out her phone as she took the two seats across the aisle from me. As the chalupa set off, she snapped a picture of the both of us, which she immediately posted to Facebook with the caption "Expedition on the Río Magdalena with Jordan." After two years away from Colombia, upon my return it seemed like suddenly everyone, everywhere, had smartphones in their hands—from Don Dubier in the rural highlands of Quinchana to twelve-year-old Gregory in Estación Cocorná—and they were constantly sending videos and music and photos to one another or posting on social media. Even as the chalupa zoomed through some of the more desolate stretches of the Magdalena, there was cell service, and Alejandra would be communicating with someone.

I call Alejandra "nomadic" because that's what she called herself, aiming to live a life free of long-term commitments and willing to pick up everything and move at the first hint of a possible adventure. Twenty-five years ago, at only nineteen, she quit her job as a physician's assistant and used the money from her severance to purchase ten electric sewing machines, which she'd heard were in high demand around the town of Plato, farther north along the Magdalena: "I got a room in Plato, and I went out every day with a forty-pound machine over each shoulder, and a canteen filled with creamy mamey-fruit juice beside my hip." Traveling by canoe and foot through the paramilitary-infested river towns, she sold the machines to people even if they didn't have cash, returning to her room at night with chickens and pieces of gold chains that they gave her in exchange for her goods. She told me other stories of camping on the beaches of Santa Marta, armed with only a single harpoon, subsisting on the reef fish she speared and ate with the fresh limes she gathered and the biscuits and soda she carried along in her knapsack. During what was meant to be only a brief trip with friends to Guatemala last year, she decided to stay for nine more months alone without any plans, and at the moment, she was working part-time for a friend who exported nuts from Brazil; with her, she brought along two plastic bags of spicy peanuts for the trip, one for each of us.

Apparently, the idea of my adventure was reason enough for her to agree to join me, at the very last minute, from where she was a day earlier: Cúcuta, a troubled city on the border with Venezuela, ten hours by bus from Barrancabermeja. I was still somewhat surprised. She was the friend of a friend of a friend and had no reason to come along but for the journey, as the boat would drop us off in El Banco, an unattractive port town where there was nothing to do but eat river fish and shop for knickknacks made in China. I was to continue by land to the old colonial town of Mompox, even farther out of the way. I was not sure what her plans were. Strapped to her backpack, she carried a camping tent, "just in case." This alone made me nervous.

Her very presence mostly assuaged my safety concerns, though— for while I was surely no match for a paramilitary militia in the case of a riverside stranding, she surely was. On her right forearm was what looked like a massive, wrinkled scar, a large round deformity just below her elbow; I wondered to myself what it could have been from. She had a strong, muscular build and carried herself with an air of indestructible confidence, knowing almost instinctively whom to trust, and whom to not. Her intelligence and intuition were paramount, and she seemed to know exactly what I was thinking before the words could escape my lips. And she was company—knowledgeable company at that, having briefly worked for Ecopetrol on the Magdalena many years ago, and having spent so much time traveling along its banks. I was more than grateful to have her along.

Our chalupa was a rickety old thing, I realized from the sight of the cockroaches and from the thunderous sound of what felt like splitting wood every time the boat hit a wave and crashed back down onto the surface of the water. Like all modes of transportation in Colombia, it was decorated extravagantly: its bright green, red, and yellow paint job (with bombastic, flowing script reading, TRANS-PORTES SAN PABLO, the name of the ferry company) and luggage tied precariously to its bouncing roof nearly looked like an amphibious version of the chiva buses that plied the steep mountain roads of the Andean southwest.

Puerto Wilches, 7:15 a.m.

APPROACHING PUERTO WILCHES, THE CITYSCAPE FELL away, and the plantations began. Oil palms stretched east and west of the river in uniform rows, intermixing with slender papaya and leafy mango trees near the water. A solitary campesino stood at the edge of the brush, overlooking the river as the rising sun illuminated the face beneath his baseball cap. A flat, wooden planchón ferry, pushed by a tugboat, passed us by—on it were five cattle lorries, an oil tanker, a yellow taxi, and two trucks loaded with spiky palm fruits the color of blood, which would be pressed to yield the palm oil that has become so ubiquitous in our processed foods and beauty products at the expense of tropical forests around the world.

"The river has these powerful currents," Alejandra had explained to me as we were picking up speed, though out of my back window I couldn't see much except the spray we were leaving behind. "They stir beneath the surface, churning up logs of great sizes that could damage the boat. But the captains know how to read the water, they've been doing this for generations."

We arrived about forty minutes after setting off from Barrancabermeja, and the five-minute stop at the small port of the village was chaotic. On the dock, peddlers selling bags of kettle corn and large bunches of dried plantains screamed through the open-air windows of the chalupa, hoping for their best possible chance at a sale for the day. At the river's edge, four barefoot boys sat upon an embankment, eating juicy-looking pieces of fruit out of thin plastic shopping bags. A few passengers disembarked, and several new ones took their places.

Alejandra pulled out a map she'd drawn on graph paper. I was growing increasingly surprised at how much she'd prepared for this. As we made our way downriver, she said, we would be passing through very isolated areas, and the stops on the chalupa would get farther apart until El Banco. She'd marked them down in capital letters—PUERTO WILCHES, CANTAGALLO, SAN PABLO, VIJAGUAL, GAMARRA, LA GLORIA, EL BANCO—as well as many of the major geographical markers: the San Lucas Mountains, the entrance to the Zapatosa Marsh and the Mompox Depression, tributary rivers, smaller settlements, and more. "The people who live here have very few resources," she explained to me. "And they've suffered a lot over the years."

It's true that the towns along this stretch of the Magdalena Medio, so resource rich yet immensely isolated from the authority of the central government of Colombia, have been some of the hardest hit by the violence. A recently declassified 1983 U.S. embassy report on violence in the Magdalena Medio outlined the various guerrilla, paramilitary, and other armed groups that operated in the area—like Embrion, a two-hundred-strong group of paramilitaries active in the 1980s, mostly in the rural swaths of land between Puerto Wilches and the southern reaches of Barrancabermeja, known for seizing and murdering its victims in broad daylight (especially on Sundays) and then throwing their bodies into the Magdalena River. "MANY, IF NOT MOST, OF THE INHABITANTS, ESPECIALLY IN THE COUNTRYSIDE, HAVE EITHER SUPPORTED THE GUERRILLAS OUT OF CONVICTION OR HAVE COLLABORATED WITH THEM OUT OF FEAR," declared the typewritten embassy report. Indeed, the communist rebels exploited the suffering of the landless campesinos in recruitment efforts, even going as far as threatening families to turn over children to join their ranks. In the Magdalena Medio, guerrilla groups like the ELN—the same group that courted Father López Arroyave's followers after the paramilitary massacre in Estación Cocorná—made it their goal to sabotage the country's oil industry, relentlessly bombing pipelines and other fossil-fuel infrastructure. That led U.S. petroleum corporations and other powerful extractionist entities to join the wealthy ranchers and drug traffickers in supporting their eradication. The Colombian military wasn't opposed to the presence of paramilitaries, either—long accused of tolerating them, even actively collaborating with them— as they bolstered its own attempts to wipe out the guerrillas.

And so, towns like Puerto Wilches saw this all-encompassing battle playing out in their backyards: on their plantations, in their pastures, and in their streets. The river was the dumping ground of choice, as always, and without much government attention, the Magdalena Medio slumbered on through a nightmare.

Cantagallo, 7:30 a.m.

A MAZE OF RIVER ISLANDS LAY BETWEEN PUERTO WILCHES, on the Magdalena's eastern bank, and the town of Cantagallo, across the way on the western bank. The town of roughly eight thousand people relied more on river than road and thus had far more boats along its wharf than its eastern-bank counterpart. There was even an ambulance chalupa. Meanwhile, the local sand diggers, half a dozen bare-chested men, were out in full force beside the Cantagallo dock.

They didn't bring a dump truck down to the river's edge, like in Girardot. In fact, the erosion of the riverbank created a ledge so dramatic that this was impossible. They hoisted wheelbarrows filled with sediment along a system of staggered wooden planks until reaching the top, solid ground, where they pushed the loads over the ledge and out of view.

"They make a bit more than one hundred dollars per dump-truck-load of sand."

I turned around. An older man sitting near me had noticed I was staring. "Changing the river like that . . ." He trailed off, shaking his head, as if to ask, *Is it worth it?* A few moments later: "I'll tell you, I live in Pinillos, Bolívar, up near El Banco, and work as a mechanic in Barranca. I've been traveling this route for fifteen years, and every time, the river is different."

Alejandra started up a fervent conversation with the man. They began by sharing stories of his hometown of Pinillos, which she knew well, and by the end were discussing the possibility of starting a business together. This was Alejandra's life. Meanwhile, I was enthralled by the view out my window—after Cantagallo, the river began to widen and split into branches meandering around masses of green, giving the chalupa captain a difficult choice of several possible routes to take before they all converged about a mile farther north. Frequently the motor would snag, grumbling with sediment, and the captain would curse. Too shallow. He stopped the boat multiple times, turning it around in order to seek out a deeper channel that would take us where we needed to go. The passengers were used to it and did not react; the jolting of the boat back and forth hardly woke them from their naps.

San Pablo, 7:50 a.m.

VERY FEW PEOPLE, I SOON REALIZED, OFTEN TOOK THIS chalupa as far as we were planning to go. At San Pablo, about half of the thirty passengers got off the boat, and I took a vacant seat farther up on the left side before we pushed off for the first of several longer legs of the trip. It would be an hour to the next stop, Vijagual.

We rounded a bend, and the river stretched out to the horizon, a straight line ahead of flat, expansive water and dazzling bright-green banks basking in the glow of the fresh August sun. I thought about how, fifty years ago, with dense forests on either side of a shadowy river, this vista would have hardly existed; these days, the canopies were withdrawn, only visible farther inland to the west, where tall, tree-blanketed mountains still loomed in their majesty, engulfed by ominous clouds and sheets of twinkling rain.

"The Serranía de San Lucas, southern Bolívar Department," Alejandra announced, though this time I didn't need the heads-up: The San Lucas mountain range, a vast ridge between the Cauca and Magdalena Rivers, remains one of the most complicated conflict zones in the country. Few regions of the megabiodiverse Colombian countryside are also thought to be home to more plant and animal species—discovered or undiscovered—than the heavily forested knot of rolling hills and gushing streams of the San Lucas. I thought back to Quinchana and San Agustín in southwestern Huila's great Colombian Massif—in many ways, the San Lucas Mountains were a living snapshot of its past, with river gorges as roads and guerrilla soldiers hidden away in the hills. This was still very much the reality in the isolated San Lucas, where networks of dirt roads and transient mining settlements deep in the forest have long made it easy for various criminal groups to clash over territory and resources without much government intervention.

It often happens that the most biodiverse and resource-rich lands are also the most brutally contested, and the San Lucas Mountains are no different. When massive gold reserves were discovered in the 1990s, the sleepy village of Santa Rosa del Sur—set amid a maze of wetlands a dozen miles inland from the Magdalena—became a boomtown for illegal miners, a gateway into the hills. Wildlife activists immediately lamented the uncontrolled exploitation of land as "a massive environmental and human catastrophe on an unimaginable scale." The runoff of mercury, sodium cyanide, oil, acetol, and formaldehyde—all chemicals used in gold extraction—drained untreated into the basins of the great Magdalena and Cauca Rivers.

At the same time, the San Lucas Mountains became just one example of the environment's role in war, both as a weapon and as a victim. Guerrilla forces relied on dense forests and disorienting wildernesses like these for cover and protection, and it was therefore in their best interests to prevent the clearing of trees for timber and mining wherever possible. In the San Lucas, sensing looming encroachment, the ELN—and, to a lesser extent, the FARC—undertook some of the stricter efforts of forest protection and land management in Colombia's modern history, declaring quasi reserves on the hillsides, outlawing deforestation, and discouraging mining settlements on land they controlled. Yet the rebel groups were far from upstanding environmental heroes, more interested in protecting themselves, and were quick to permit exploitation that would benefit them. All across Colombia, the FARC taxed the cultivation and trafficking of coca leaves, a major driver of deforestation; the ELN's environmental "enforcement" tactics were often violent, at gunpoint, threatening communities into picking up garbage and maintaining tree cover. Far from promoting any real notion of long-term "conservation," in some cases the guerrillas effectively attached a stigma to legitimate conservation campaigns that might be carried out with local communities in the future, in their absence.

Indeed, with the FARC largely demobilized since 2016, a new-found ability to explore vast tracts of its old territory has brought wide-ranging challenges. Biologists have jumped at the chance to explore new corners of the second-most biodiverse country on the planet, racing to discover new species and to conserve others already known to be threatened. At the same time, the now-unregulated passage of illegal loggers and gold miners into rural swaths of land like the San Lucas and the Amazon has caused deforestation to skyrocket across the country since the peace deal—up 60 percent between 2015 and 2018 and remaining stubbornly persistent. The cultivation of coca crops, the key ingredient for cocaine and another driver of forest loss, has reached all-time highs. And a lack of government support in newly vacated rural areas has allowed a complex web of criminal groups to rise to the occasion, wrestling for control of the resource-rich lands and lucrative smuggling corridors, in a decentralized power struggle that proves to be one of the greatest challenges facing Colombia's most rural communities as a wobbly peace moves forth.

Vijagual, 8:50 a.m.

IT SEEMED AS THOUGH I HAD A KNACK FOR MAKING friends with boatmen named Álvaro. Indeed, as our boat further emptied with each stop, I made my way closer to the front to sit with the captain—not a young man like Alvarito of Estación Cocorná but an older, soft-spoken gentleman who reminded me more of Oscar Castilla at the Hotel Pipatón or Luis Manuel Salamanca in the highlands.

His name was Álvaro Gulloso, and he never took off his sunglasses. His assistant had fallen asleep between this stop and the last, waking up briefly to hoist some bags onto the dock, but as soon as we pushed back from Vijagual for our next leg of ninety minutes, he conked out once more, and I seized my opportunity.

The driver's seat was in the front corner of the chalupa, on a raised stool in front of a window that looked far too smudged to be safe—but he looked like he knew what he was doing. I sat in the doorway beside him, facing the rest of the passengers, who watched me incredulously as I tried to strike up a conversation. The oncoming wind blew ferociously at the back of my head, and at the captain's warning, I had to hold on to a small metal handle beside my head whenever he slowed down, so as not to fly out into the river and be run over by the boat itself.

"This river is dying," was the first thing Álvaro Gulloso said to me. "Before, there were manatees, caimans, you used to see them so often! But the river is drying up now, and things are changing."

This river is dying. Later in the day, a group of fishermen in the town of El Banco would give striking color to this observation.

The beach where they congregated was a five-minute motorcycle taxi ride from the dock, down a bumpy dirt road. It was a rotten and filthy place, reeking of the garbage that was piled high along the gray sand—of course, the trash would all be swept away by the river when it rose again in a few months, with the coming of the October rains. Amid the mess, a few fishermen stood beside a large net that was drying out from that morning's outing. Many were shirtless, their dry, blistered skin in perpetual suffering from one day after the next out on the water. Their situation, they said, was grave: There was less and less rain each year, one regional effect of global climate change, which meant less water in the river, and worse fishing. Dry seasons were especially difficult, when the fish were few and families sometimes had to go without eating. So the immediate respite from hunger was always at the forefront of their minds, they said, even if it meant using destructive techniques—like dynamite, or nets with holes so small that they caught baby fish—that would ultimately lead to the quickening degradation of the ecosystem and worsening future hunger spells for their children, who would inevitably become fishermen too.

Álvaro Gulloso had been watching the river change, day by day, over the course of more than two decades—he'd been driving this route, nine total hours one way, just about every day for nearly twenty-five years. He lived in Magangué, three hours by river north of El Banco, but spent every other night in a hotel in Barrancabermeja before the chalupa departed again for Magangué at six o'clock the next morning. He'd acquired an instinctual knowledge of the river, never relying on any sort of technology on the boat to gauge the varying depths of the water at any given time. "It's something that's just drilled into your memory," he told me. "But generally, the shallower parts are flatter, smoother at the surface. The deeper parts have color, movement, character."

During the height of the war, he said, armed groups used to stand on the shores of the river, waving down the boat to take inventory of passengers and request bribes from the captains for safe passage. The river itself carried reminders of the conflict in its journey toward the sea. "During the war you'd see bunches of four or five bodies, corpses, floating in the river," Álvaro said. "Eleven was the most I ever saw at once. Eleven corpses. Imagine that. Sometimes you'd only see a head or an arm passing by. That's war."

We passed a tugboat barge slumbering beside a wide embankment. "How long do you think it has been there?" I asked. "Days?"

Álvaro laughed out loud. "Months!" he said. "The workers stay there, sleeping and eating, waiting for the river to rise again."

Gamarra, 10:20 a.m.

GAMARRA WAS THE FIRST MAGDALENA TOWN I REMEMBER reading about. It was mentioned so often in the history books and adventure accounts that I was somewhat surprised to find it not much more than an underwhelming embankment under construction. Cranes were everywhere, from the wharf farther back to several buildings that were visible from the small window out the side of the chalupa. Alejandra, Álvaro, and some of the other passengers agreed that the town was remodeling its railroad station, to accommodate the passenger train that would someday triumphantly return from

Santa Marta, but no one had the slightest idea if that would happen anytime soon.

The scenery following Gamarra was tremendous. Hundreds of cormorants flocked to the wide sandbanks where the caimans used to rest. Solitary brown eagles soared high above the flat water, while white herons with dangling legs skimmed the surface. Álvaro pointed out the trees: the umbrellalike samán, the towering ceiba, the thick-trunked oak of the tropics, and the numerous stubby palms and mangos interspersed throughout. To the northeast loomed the green, fractured peaks of the Serranía de Los Motilones, part of the eastern Andes range, and now in full view to the west appeared the dark hills of the San Lucas.

We passed another long barge, a famous one: the *Humberto Muñoz R.*, named for the man known as the "father of Colombian shipping," one of the Magdalena's most legendary steamboatmen and the founder of the Naviera Fluvial Colombiana (NFC; Colombian Shipping Company). Álvaro pointed the chalupa straight toward it and gunned the engine. The multistory tugboat painted red and white pushed a barge longer than a football field that was piled high with coal. The Giant of the Magdalena, as it was nicknamed, became the first of its kind to ply the Magdalena River when the NFC commissioned it in Muñoz's memory in 2010, at the start of the country's resurgent hopes for transport along the river.

We stopped alongside the tugboat, and one of our passengers quietly rose from his seat. A deckhand from the *Humberto Muñoz R.* extended his hand, and the passenger climbed out of the front windshield and onto the larger vessel—presumably to begin his shift for the slow, difficult slog back upriver.

La Gloria (Cesar), 11:05 a.m.

THINGS BEGAN TO SLOW BY LA GLORIA, IN THE CESAR DE-
partment, as the day grew long and the distance between the stops
even longer.

"Do you want to know what happened to my arm?" Alejandra
asked me out of the blue. "I saw that you noticed it earlier but didn't
say anything."

I stammered as I tried to lie my way around the fact that she was
exactly right. "Wow," I said finally. "I didn't see it before."

"I thought I saw you look at it and then turn away."

"Well, then," I replied, still avoiding a confession, "what happened?"

"I died once," she said very matter-of-factly. I almost choked on
my spicy Brazilian peanut.

"I'm sorry?"

"I died once." She was sixteen years old, she said, and she was
driving a car with her friend in the passenger seat. Her friend told her
to speed up to catch a car farther ahead of them. She didn't want to
do it. He insisted. She wasn't going to listen to him, and then he took
his left foot and pressed hard on her accelerator himself, thrusting
the car forward.

Alejandra's immediate reaction was to slam on the brakes. The
pressure of both the gas and the brakes on the tires was too much.
One tire exploded, and the car spun out of control, slamming into a
light post. The streetlamp fell onto the car, shattering the windshield,
gashing Alejandra's forearm, and puncturing her lungs. Her pelvis
shattered, causing her organs to elevate. She blacked out and stopped
breathing. "My heart shifted position," she said.

"You know how they say that when you die, you see the light?" She asked me this seriously, with pauses long enough for the chaotic sounds of the chalupa motor to fill the silence, and I nodded. "Well," she continued, "I did not see the light, but what I did see in my dream was a doctor, dressed in all white, who came to me and asked, 'How are you feeling?'

"'I'm very thirsty,' I said. And he said, 'What do you want?'

"I said, 'A Coca-Cola.' And he took out some money and put it in a nurse's pocket, and he told her, 'Go get her a Coca-Cola.' The nurse took the money and walked away.

"And then the doctor said something to me that I would never forget, I'll never forget the way that he said it: 'You mustn't go to sleep. You have to stay awake.' The doctor said to me, 'You have to stay awake for the Coca-Cola.'

"And so I waited for what seemed like a thousand years, for an eternity. But the Coca-Cola never came. The next thing I knew, I'd awoken in the hospital, with real doctors all around me. I'd been revived, brought back from the dead.

"'Where's the Coca-Cola?' I asked my mother, who had already said goodbye to me, had already begun to agonize over my death. She did not know what I meant by it, and so I didn't mention it again. I took it as a second opportunity on earth."

"Races condemned to one hundred years of solitude did not have *a second opportunity on earth*." I could not forget those words, for they were the last of *One Hundred Years of Solitude*, Colombia's greatest novel, a prophetic story by García Márquez about the destiny of a family and the cyclical nature of time. But in his 1982 Nobel Prize acceptance speech, "The Solitude of Latin America," the great author amended the idea, hoping instead for "a new and sweeping utopia of life, where no one will be able to decide for others how they die, where love will prove true and happiness be possible, and where the races condemned to one hundred years of solitude will have, at last and forever, a second opportunity on earth."

Alejandra's story was one of survival, and her life after death has been nothing but a mission to make the most of her second chance. I figured that now was Colombia's second chance, too.

El Banco, 12:15 p.m.

AS THE NATURE-RICH, VIOLENCE-PLAGUED SERRANÍA DE San Lucas fell out of view behind us, the Magdalena lost its form, widening almost like a vast lake that didn't seem to have a beginning or end. This was the Depresión Momposina, a network of swamps and marshes that flooded and dried with the comings and goings of the rains. The river branched out into a network of ever-shifting arms, dozens of them meandering through the wetlands, trying to find some semblance of shape or direction. One of the branches passed by Mompox, the start of the Lower Magdalena.

El Banco, where Alejandra and I disembarked, was a grim port town that reminded me of Puerto Boyacá (and suffered from a similarly brutal paramilitary legacy, marked by warlords with names like Knife and Tiger and Don Mario). By no means did we intend to stay; it was simply a gateway for onward land transport to Mompox and other towns in the Bolívar and Magdalena Departments. Dozens of aggressive touts mobbed the dock with the arrival of our chalupa, grabbing our arms as we squeezed through them with our bags. They followed us into a dockside restaurant, where we took seats at a table and tried to ignore their shouts offering us motorcycle rides and lottery tickets. Behind them, I saw Álvaro Gulloso's chalupa sputter up and pull away, bound for Magangué.

Though we were still hundreds of miles from the Caribbean coast, El Banco was considered the start of the Colombian Caribbean, a region of endless banana plantations, thumping cumbia music, and large populations of Afro- and Arab Colombians.

Three stout Afro-Colombian women prepared the food in this restaurant: one, at the front, scaled and gutted bucketfuls of slimy bocachico fish, and the other two worked over crackling fryers and steaming tubs of sancocho stews and soups. One man sheepishly approached them for a slight change to his dish, and they screamed him out of the shop. I went for a yucca-and-vegetables soup and some salty grilled beef, while Alejandra opted for the deep-fried bocachico with rice and salad.

"¡Qué ricooo!" Alejandra took a photo of her foot-long fish steaming on the plate. I wondered how anyone with a choice in the matter could eat a river fish from the Magdalena anymore—especially this far downriver, where the sheer quantity of shit and sludge amassed by the flowing water was nothing short of nauseating. Then again, the beef I ordered was one of the principal reasons why Alejandra's bocachico was probably so tainted. From the crowd of hawkers emerged a small, emaciated girl asking for food, and Alejandra and I gave her pieces of bocachico and meat and some French fries.

———

WE PARTED WAYS AT A SHARE-TAXI STAND; ALEJANDRA
had decided to take her wanderings to Santa Marta, on the coast,
where her sister lived. She gave me a warm, affectionate hug. "Don't
change," she said, "and if you ever need me, I'm never more than a few
hours away. None of us are anymore, not in this world." And with
that, she hopped into the back of a jeep that was pulling away and
she was gone.

I was heading to Mompox, two hours away from El Banco by
pickup truck. The people at the share-taxi stand pointed me to a
white one and said it would be leaving "ahorita."

I groaned. "Ahorita" had already easily become my least favorite
expression in Colombian Spanish, as it could mean anything from
"right now" to "a little while from now" to "a little while ago." It was one
of the many things that made public transportation nothing short of
a comical affair in the country. Though long-distance-bus timetables
were posted at the stations, people laughed in your face if you tried to
make a fuss. Names of transportation companies, like Cootransmag
and Cootraimar, were dizzying abbreviations that somehow made
things more difficult to understand, and it didn't matter where you
were traveling in the country, because every driver from every company loved the same slow, romantic accordion music that they blasted
at full volume, making sleeping impossible.

In this case, I braced myself for what "ahorita" could mean. It
would all depend on how long it would take to fill the remaining
seats in the car, to ensure the driver earned his money's worth for the
trip. So long as there was an empty seat, we weren't going anywhere;
there were two left besides mine. The driver was a tall, older Black

man who gave me no further information besides "ahorita" and told me his name was El Negro—a common Spanish nickname that, in cases like this, does not carry the same racist connotations it does in English.

El Negro, his assistant driver, and I set off from the share-taxi stand and drove aimlessly about the town, honking our horn at random townspeople in the hopes that they were in need of a ride to Mompox or points in between. This did not work, but it gave El Negro a good laugh.

We then made our way to the main bus terminal of El Banco, a large complex with double-decker coach buses heading to places like Medellín and Bogotá on long, seventeen-hour roundabout routes. El Negro parked on the street out front, and the three of us sat under the shade of a tree on the sidewalk. The two Colombians started barking at passersby: "Mompox, Guamal, Mompox, Guamal, two seats for Mompox or Guamal..." They laughed when I joined in after an hour, out of desperation.

A woman paid the drivers ten dollars to have several heavy boxes of toilet paper, hardware, and fruit transported in our truck to Mompox. I helped carry everything to the car for free. The three of us all cursed under our breath when we found out she would not be accompanying her freight on the ride. I counted one, two, three double-decker buses leaving the terminal for faraway cities before we even found one more passenger to join us. It occurred to me that I could probably just walk into the terminal and find another share-taxi to take me to Mompox that might fill up faster, but I was starting to feel a sense of camaraderie with El Negro and his assistant at this point. The sun lowered in the sky as the afternoon wore on, and the birds began to sing their sunset songs. It was comfortably warm out, not oppressively so. We happened to be sitting on the stoop of a bakery, and I downed two bags of water and three pastries filled with guayaba jam during our wait. Finally, miraculously, an older woman and her granddaughter bought the remaining two seats. After three hours of "ahorita," we set off.

Mompox was reached by a difficult, unpaved road that wound through wetlands and pastures. Guamal was the only other significant settlement along the way, a collection of a few colorful homes among very dusty dirt paths. Many people in Guamal wore face masks or lifted damp towels to their noses whenever a car rumbled by, which I hadn't seen elsewhere in Colombia. We passed two cocks fighting unaccompanied in the street, and in avoiding them we very nearly ran over one of the skinny dogs that lay at the road's edge.

During the ride, El Negro repeatedly attempted to show off his English skills.

"My name is Jordan," I said, slowly, to demonstrate.

"Mai nayme ees ... El Negro!" he echoed, and the rest of us in the car burst out laughing. We repeated this same routine many times, and nobody seemed to tire of it.

He requested I play music from my country on his car stereo. He knew "Hotel California" and found it amusing that we listened to the same kind of music—me all the way in New York and him on the road between El Banco and Mompox. In his excitement, he proceeded to ask me which vallenato songs were the most popular in the United States. I fumbled over a polite response that would not break his heart.

As we drove northwest, the sun was setting over the deep-green marshlands and pastures of the Depresión Momposina. We crossed a new, paved bridge over the Mompox branch of the Magdalena. El Negro crossed his chest and said, "Welcome to God's country."

PART THREE

Bajo Magdalena

Lower Magdalena

10

The Master Jeweler

AN OLD MAN NAMED SIMÓN VILLANUEVA LAY A THREAD of shiny silver wire atop his wooden workbench. He cut the strand into six pieces and used pincers to twirl them into tiny, tightly wound bulbs no larger than small beads before carefully wedging each of them into the frame of a six-petal flower.

"I've gotten used to having poor vision," Simón said as he put on his thick, black-rimmed glasses. The oldest jeweler in town had been perfecting his craft for decades and had largely learned to work with just his hands at this point—an ability that served him well as his vision faded with age. He was eighty-nine years old when I met him, but, like everyone in Santa Cruz de Mompox, he looked many years younger. And still, he was able to twist and plait fine strands of silver to produce the looping, intricate designs of his imagination: little fish earrings, a bracelet with a flower pendant, a necklace carrying a small sombrero vueltiao. No two pieces were the same, and he kept hundreds of his glittering, unsold creations in a glass case on shelves laden with red velvet padding.

His style of jewelry is called filigree, and Mompox is one of only a few places in South America where it is still regularly practiced as an industry. Thought to have originated in Mesopotamia and Egypt several thousand years ago, filigree followed the great migrations of humans to the empires of ancient Greece and Rome and to the dynasties of East Asia and India, where it is most commonly found today. So, too, did it follow the Muslim conquests from the Middle East into North Africa and the Iberian Peninsula in the seventh and eighth centuries, becoming widespread in present-day Spain and Portugal during hundreds of years of Islamic rule. Filigree is just a hint of pervasive Arabic and Eastern influence on Hispanic culture and society; seeing the grand mosques and flamenco dances of Andalusia even today, one is more consciously aware of the traces of Damascus and Baghdad and the Sindh.

In turn, like so much else of the Arab Spanish blend, filigree made its way to Mompox during the colonization of Latin America in the sixteenth and seventeenth centuries. It made sense: Mompox was a goldsmith's town, a major Spanish colonial outpost founded in 1537 and strategically located on the Magdalena River during the days of the gold and silver trade. Merchandise coming from the mines of Colombia's interior was prepared for the river journey to the Caribbean coast, where it would be placed on ships bound for Europe and the rest of the world. A royal mint was established in Mompox, where the abundant precious metals were taxed at a rate of 20 percent by the Spanish (the "royal fifth"), and the town became known as the City of Gold.

But Simón Villanueva did not come from a lavish life of riches and jewels; no, his grandmother came to Mompox from Margarita, a nearby village known for cultivating oranges and other citrus fruits. Born in 1928, Simón got his start with filigree at the age of twelve, learning first from a few uncles while selling soup from his family's doorstep and then from an apprenticeship with Luis Guillermo Tres Palacios, whom he called "the greatest goldsmith Mompox has ever seen." In this way he quietly found his place in a tradition that has journeyed and endured for more than four millennia.

"You don't think about time when you're doing this," he said to me as he put together the small silver flower, not larger than a quarter. It was a solitary craft; his area consisted of only a rocking chair and his jeweler's table on the covered front porch of his red-and-green house, where he worked from six in the morning to six in the evening, when he couldn't anymore for lack of light. He lived on a loud, social block—street vendors passed by at all hours hawking fresh cheese and meat, and motorcycles rumbled through on their way to the main town square. An elderly woman who appeared much older than Simón sat in her own rocking chair on the porch across the street, beneath hanging wicker baskets for sale, gazing off into the distance and not really interacting with anyone but for the occasional smile she sent his way. Simón remembered when a group of itinerant Romany people sold horses from tents on a nearby corner in the 1950s, and when Syrian and Lebanese immigrants delivered textile products door to door. All of this had, for years, easily distracted him from his work, but that was part of the fun; as absorbed as he might have been in completing a particular, delicate design, he never failed to look up with a smile to return someone's greeting from across the way.

There's a certain kind of romanticized image one expects when meeting someone like Simón—the oldest, most well-regarded jeweler in a small town, who spends his days honing an antiquated art from a faraway land. I'd envisioned a slender, delicate man, perhaps, with fine fingers. When I found him seated on his porch for the first time, however, he was corpulent and shirtless, wearing only a pair of faded white shorts with a permanently broken zipper. Part of his stomach protruded from the opening of his fly, and the rest of his body sagged over the sides of the chair in layers (the next day, he'd upgraded to a pressed, blue-and-white-striped button-down shirt, with short sleeves and a large breast pocket). His hair was white and unkempt, and he had a gray, bushy mustache that reached the corners of his mouth. He spoke quickly, in a raspy, slurred Spanish that was difficult for me to understand because of his lack of teeth.

But in so many other ways, he fit the mold. His workbench was an eighty-year-old antique that he planned to take to the grave. "To work in heaven," he said, laughing gently. Whenever he spoke about his filigree, his face broke into a wide smile. "I live in love with my work," he said over and over again. "I live in love with my work." He was as prolific and revered a goldsmith as any in Mompox and throughout Colombia, and from his chair he'd watched his town change over the course of three-quarters of a century.

———

MORNINGS IN THE OLD QUARTER OF MOMPOX SEEMED LIKE they could have been the same for hundreds of years. The cobblestone streets yawned at eight o'clock with the occasional pedestrian but didn't really get going until nine or nine thirty. Suddenly, they bustled with men, young and old, riding horse-drawn carts. The carts far outnumbered the occasional bicycle taxi or motorcycle, which still scared the giant iguanas back into the protection of the shady trees and vegetation that lined one side of the main riverside drag, La Albarrada, known in the past as, among other names, La Albarrada de los Turcos (the Street of the Turks). The gloomy Brazo de Mompox, the town's branch of the Magdalena, flowed slowly and sadly alongside La Albarrada, and I watched as an old man in a wooden canoe paddled across the river. His boat carried three schoolgirls in red-and-white-checkered skirts into town from the farmhouse across the way.

Most, if not all, of the changes that have befallen Mompox have been related in one way or another to this branch of the Magdalena, which was apparently once much wider and fuller, engulfing the pastures that now lay so close to the town on the opposite bank of the river. Until recently, the Magdalena's Brazo de Mompox was the only way to reach the town at all. Spanish explorers used it to access the interior of the country from the coast, resulting in the founding of Mompox and its enrichment from the gold and silver trade in the years that followed. Commerce followed the riches, filling the river with canoes, rafts, and—beginning in the nineteenth century—steamboats. The steamboats were the new gold of the Magdalena, with their towering smokestacks and three-story decks carrying passengers enjoying restaurants, bakeries, and orchestras that played until sunrise. Mompox was an important stop along the route from the capital to the coast, which could easily take weeks. It was a place where passengers could rest for the night and the vessels could resupply and refuel.

Some who arrived via the Magdalena never left, and in the late nineteenth and early twentieth centuries Mompox saw a flood of Middle Eastern migrants seeking economic opportunity. Families with names like Hazbun, El-Hadwe, and Abuabara arrived in Mompox from the Levant, escaping religious persecution as Christian and Jewish minorities living under the Islamic rule of the Ottoman Empire. The "turcos," as they were widely known, mistakenly and sometimes derogatorily, for traveling under Ottoman Turkish passports (remember Mompox's Street of the Turks), settled throughout Latin America during this period—indeed, my own great-grandparents, members of Syria's centuries-old Jewish community, fled to Buenos Aires in the early 1900s. It was not difficult for me to imagine my ancestors arriving in Colombia instead of Argentina, to picture my great-grandfather working as a traveling salesman by boat along the Río Magdalena instead of on horseback along the spine of the southern Andes.

Whether in Buenos Aires, Panama City, or Mompox, seemingly everywhere the "turcos" went they established textile businesses similar to those that brought them great success in the old days of the Silk Road, from multinational fabric companies to itinerant peddling routes and small shops covered floor to ceiling with colorful bedsheets and cloths. In Mompox, ninety-three-year-old Faride Khalilieh still owned the Dau Textile Shop, the last of its kind remaining in town, where she and her son Eddie sold sheets, pants, underwear, and shoes; her father, Yiris Khalilieh, arrived in Mompox on a steamboat in 1919, hailing from the Palestinian Christian town of Beit Jala, near Bethlehem. Just down the road was a corner store selling kibbe burghul—fried balls of spiced ground meat, onions, pine nuts, and cracked wheat—and other dishes popular in the Levant. An influx of Germans and other Europeans accompanied the Middle Easterners, and the result was a vibrant atmosphere of commerce and transport among locals and new immigrants, both on the river and in the town that ran alongside it.

Enter Simón Villanueva, who as a young man would meet the docking steamboats in the 1940s and '50s—heading upriver on Mondays, downriver on Wednesdays, he remembered—to sell his jewelry to the disembarking passengers. His customers traveled in luxury, he said, wearing white suits and drinking wine on their way between Bogotá and the coast on the grandiose vessels. In 1946, aged eighteen, he boarded a steamboat himself, bound for a better life in the coastal city of Barranquilla, taking his jeweler's workbench and supplies along with him. But the promise of the big city, for him, turned out to be a great illusion; for several years he struggled before realizing that Mompox was where he belonged. Five years after he initially set out from home, he returned. He married his wife that year, in 1951, and together they moved into the house where he'd remained ever since.

As it happened, those passengers turned out to be among Mompox's last: a combination of sedimentation and other environmental changes in the 1960s and '70s caused the network of Magdalena River branches to shift their positions away from Mompox. The Mompox branch narrowed and dried, and another branch welled up farther away, taking over as the main arm of the Magdalena for good. Far from any airport and, until recently, without a connection to most major roads, Mompox suddenly lost its link to the rest of the country, left with nothing more than a narrow waterway that now looked more like a shallow creek than one of the great rivers of the Americas. In a way, though, the timing of the shift helped save Mompox from the worst of the war—and as the country grew increasingly paralyzed, Mompox was relatively isolated from the violence. Had it remained a port of strategic importance, surely things would have been different, and far more destructive. Instead, for nearly fifty years, it felt as if nobody came in or out.

These days, every person, every building, brought reminders of the days of old. I spent many days and nights roaming Mompox, with its quiet corridors and slow-going riverside cafés, its trees raining fresh fruit in abundance. Stores closed each afternoon to make way for long siestas during the heat of the day; the streets bustled anew only after the sun went down. Sometimes, during these hours of rest, families would invite me in for a cup of coffee or a dewy glass of ice-cold corozo juice, which we would drink stretched out in hammocks or rocking chairs. Their homes were magnificent, stately places—long and narrow with open-air hallways running alongside rectangular courtyards of palm fronds and flowering plants neatly organized among beds of stones—guarded by tall wooden doors opened with heavy black keys. Many were descendants of the businessmen and aristocrats of centuries past; some even told me that they were heirs of Spanish nobles called marquesas, living off of their ancestors' fortunes in servant-filled mansions facing the river.

Beyond the legendary old quarter, past the main asphalt road and far from the Magdalena, was another side to Mompox that most visitors would not reach—poorer peripheral neighborhoods like Barrio Faciolince, where the houses were much smaller and more run down, and where the dirt lanes were nearly impassable after most major rainstorms. Here lived various descendants of some of Mompox's orig-

inal residents, like a sixty-five-year-old woodworker named Samuel
Mármol Villa, better known as Don Abundio—a third-generation
folklorist working to preserve the age-old African and Indigenous tra-
ditions of the Caribbean coast through music and dance. "Ours is an
amphibious culture," he said as he showed me a collection of wooden
flutes, artisanal drums, and handmade animal masks depicting the
various species that once lived abundantly in the surrounding forests
and wetlands. "Just about everything we do is connected to the Río
Magdalena—the river that built this country will, if things continue,
destroy this country, too." Just as it had forgotten Mompox.

But Mompox, in all of its solitude, was indeed a magical place—
people said this to me over and over again when I told them I would
be going. At every chance, the town gave you the feeling that it was
a place touched by God, if such a place existed. Each night, as if on
a schedule, bats descended on the dimly lit streets and glowing pla-
zas, fluttering in and out of the open doors of the sixteenth-century
churches and underneath the sweeping arches of the grand Spanish
colonial homes. The blue skies of the day were replaced by clouds that
rolled in like armies, ushering in a gentle evening breeze as the young
nights lit up with silent bolts of lightning. The people seemed to live
forever, all of them, well into their eighties and nineties, and in good
health, with memories that never failed them. The older ones, who
always looked younger than they were, spent evenings and nights sitting on the stoops of their homes, fanning away the mosquitoes, and
chatting with whoever was passing by, including me. Spontaneous
courtly dances erupted at the will of musicians like Don Abundio
happening upon a plaza, and there was no shortage of musicians in
the town.

———

"AN ARTISAN WITHOUT MEMORIES, WHOSE ONLY DREAM was to die of fatigue in the oblivion and misery of his little gold fishes," wrote García Márquez in *One Hundred Years of Solitude*, set in the fictional town of Macondo, which, with its Street of the Turks, wandering merchants, and filigree goldsmiths, is thought in part to be Mompox in disguise. Many of Colombia's small Caribbean towns like to claim the honor, including García Márquez's own Aracataca, but it's hard not to believe the momposinos. In the story, a man named Colonel Aureliano Buendía spends his final days at his workbench, meticulously shaping little filigree fishes, only to keep melting his creations back down and making them over again in an inescapable cycle of loneliness and dementia.

The lack of customers never stopped Simón Villanueva from making more filigree to add to his display case each day, piece by piece, like drops in a bucket. He saw himself as more of an engineer than a jeweler. "This will never end," he told me when I asked him if his was a disappearing art form, "because inventing new designs will never get old." I wondered how he fed his family with so many jewels and hardly anyone to sell them to. His creations—dazzling little fishes, sombreros, petaled flowers—piled up in his glass cabinet. But all the while the master jeweler kept working, always plaiting and coiling and welding at the same rhythmic pace, giving every piece the attention and passion it deserved before moving on to the next. There was simply nothing else he'd rather have done. For my own memory, I bought a set of delicately plated little fishes that he said he'd made just the day before. He charged me less than eight dollars, the cost of four lunches.

Simón's home was set several blocks back from the river, away from the colonial mansions with lofty doors and ceilings. Like many of the other homes in this area of town, it was brightly colored and had several street-facing windows, the yellow wood-paneled shutters open to let in any possible semblance of a breeze to alleviate the sticky heat. His six-year-old granddaughter spent each day running around her grandfather's workstation on the small porch, and I remembered Delfín Borrero and his canoes. In one of the windows, on the first day, I saw another filigree workstation, set in a dark bedroom and caked with ashen dust. A single lightbulb hung by a thin metal pipe from the ceiling, illuminating another grandchild—a young man named Luis Eduardo Villanueva—and his workbench, atop which were strewn several newly completed three-leaf earrings.

"It's a tradition," Luis Eduardo told me. "I've been learning since I was little. You do the work for your heart, not for the money. My father does it, my uncles, my cousins."

"It fills me with joy to know that I taught them and that they're continuing the practice," Simón said of his son and grandson. "They're also teaching others. That's the chain of jewelry, each one teaching the next—as they say, first you're a son, and then you're a father."

After filling the outline of his most recent design—the flower with the curved bulbs—Simón sprinkled a silver powder over the entire piece, which was no more than an inch in diameter, to give it a stronger shine. He placed it on a flat stone and took out a small, rudimentary welder, which he used to fuse the filling with the outline, creating a flower that looked almost as if it were made of silver mesh. For a few seconds after the flame was applied, the flower maintained a red, ember-like glow. Simón placed it, still soft from the heat, in a smooth mortar, and used a stone pestle to gently pound it. This caused the petals to bend upward, giving the flower a touch of life. When he was finished, he picked up the tiny object with his thick fingers and inspected it. "I didn't imagine it this way," Simón the jeweler said, slightly surprised by his new creation. "But, looking at it now, I like it."

11

Biblioburro

LUIS SORIANO WAS BORN SO PREMATURE THAT WHEN HE
arrived into the world, everyone was sure that he would die.

He was born in 1972, in the very same village of La Gloria (Magdalena Department) where he grew up and made his life. His father
was a cattle rancher, and his mother sold fruit and milk on the side of
the road. They were hardworking campesino parents who would later
emphasize, to their many children, the importance of an education
over everything else.

Luis grew up playing in the long, rolling fields of the Magdalena
valley. La Gloria was set inland from the river, by about one hour
in each of two potential directions, yet the river wielded great influence upon the town: it was built, in fact, during the golden age of
river transport, when through travelers heading toward river ports
like Mompox and Plato would inevitably stop in La Gloria for on-

ward transportation, and when farmers could easily find vessels to transport their products far across Colombia. In town, so too it was said that the Magdalena still dictated the rains and the floods of the nearby lowlands, which influenced the rains and the floods in La Gloria, and during droughts, the town felt the river's pain. The river's beaches and sandy islands yielded the yucca, plantains, and beans of the Caribbean diet—La Gloria is nearly one hundred miles from the nearest Caribbean seaside town, but yes, its people will tell you, it is indeed a Caribbean place.

Raised in the countryside, Luis learned things from the land that people from the city never understood. In the hot, humid afternoons, a line of ants hurrying across the path meant that the skies were about to open and intense rains would fall and freshen the air; at night, the sudden silence of the frogs and the toads meant that another person was approaching in the darkness. From watching the birds, he gathered certain observations about their daily routines, like which of the trees the flocks of red-and-green macaws preferred for their nightly roosts and at what hours of the day the sirirí sang its lonely song. These were things that he learned from a very young age and carried with him throughout his life.

But Colombia's escalating violence in the 1970s and '80s meant that Luis would not be able to stay. When the paramilitaries and other criminal groups plagued La Gloria and the surrounding wide-open countryside, Luis's parents sent him and his siblings to live with family in Valledupar, a departmental capital. His life playing among the animals was replaced by the loud, gritty streets of a valley city.

By the time Luis finished high school and returned to La Gloria, he decided, maybe as a product of all of this learning and absorbing in his own life, that he wanted to become a schoolteacher. He got a job in a small, rural primary school in nearby Nueva Granada, where he taught reading and writing. At the same time, he completed a remote degree from the Universidad del Magdalena.

But none of his students did any of their schoolwork or seemed to make any progress in the first few years, and Luis blamed himself for it. He thought he was a bad teacher, that he had misjudged his life's purpose, all because the students just didn't seem to be learning—until he started asking them questions, trying to figure out why it was. He realized that many of the children, living on isolated farmsteads several miles' walk along narrow dirt paths from the nearest school, couldn't practice reading at home because they didn't have access to books. A teacher with limited resources himself, he decided to do the only thing he could: bring his own books to them.

And so, before dawn one day in 1997, he took one of his donkeys and a stack of books—and like something out of a fairy tale, he set off across the countryside. Covering several miles of difficult terrain, he stopped at the homes of each one of his students and read with them, before lending them the book and telling them he'd be back the next day to pick it up. And in this manner, he returned day after day, in the early hours of morning, well before school started, for he knew from experience that families living in the fields rose with the first song of the sirirí and the crows of roosters in the dark. More than twenty years on, he hasn't stopped. "At first, people saw me as nothing more than a half-insane teacher with some books and his donkey," Luis liked to say. "Without realizing it at the time, I'd created the very same rural traveling library that the world now knows as the Biblioburro."

Biblioburro started out with just seventy books, all of them Luis's own, and only one donkey. He quickly added a second donkey, affixing wooden bookcases to both of their saddles for ease of transport, and named the two animals Alfa and Beto ("alfabeto," alphabet in Spanish). He started extending and diversifying each day's route to reach more children in the area. When the beloved Colombian national radio broadcaster Juan Gossaín got wind of the Biblioburro story in 2003 and shared it with his listeners, book donations from around the world started pouring in—today, Luis boasts a collection of more than seven thousand titles. Yet for all the international attention, it remains a humble operation. When Luis sets off on a Biblioburro visit, he does it alone, quietly, with his two trusted donkeys. Often, he won't encounter another person for hours as he makes his way across the rugged, lonesome terrain—an uncomfortable ride, and an even more arduous walk, beneath the merciless sun. But the children who live in these lonely places await the arrival of the Biblioburro and its stories with great fervor, running wide-eyed toward Alfa and Beto when they spot them emerging from the horizon. Perhaps, in the children he serves, Luis Soriano sees some part of himself. He sees that they can beat the odds—for while Luis has easily become the most famous person to ever come from La Gloria, at the moment of his birth, you would have been hard-pressed to find anyone who imagined he would have resurged from his situation as well as he did.

Except for one person, that is. As the story goes, his parents called upon an older woman, who was very respected in town, to come examine the child and give him her blessing. Minutes after Luis's birth, she made her way over to the house and stood over him, looking his tiny little body up and down, seeming to ponder whether he would be destined to live as long as she had. After several moments, she spoke. "This little one, he isn't going to die" was what the old woman said (though who knows if she actually believed it herself). "He is going to grow up and become a doctor, and he will save this town."

———

WE'D GOTTEN A LATE START THAT MORNING, FOR LUIS Soriano's motorcycle was broken, and he had to find a replacement part. I found him along the highway, bent over his old Yamaha outside a friend's auto body shop, which was actually not much more than a wooden shed inhabited by several cats and one man.

"Doctor," the man said, emerging from his cluttered shed after several minutes, and Luis looked up. He was not a doctor, despite the nickname that everyone had been calling him since his boyhood, but he did not think much of it. "You're all set."

"Gracias, amigo."

Luis, who I noticed walked with a slight limp, wheeled his newly repaired motorcycle to the side of the road and gestured for me to hop on. La Gloria, a transit town, was a two-road village, built in the 1940s when a new highway created the only intersection that could be found for miles. He drove us thirty seconds around the corner to an unmarked yellow building, across from a noisy restaurant and an even noisier school. Around this corner he was not only known as "Doctor" but "Profe"—the school, a public school, was one he founded. The adjoining restaurant was his wife's, where the smell of stews and frying meat drifted past men drinking sweating orange sodas in the shade. Without saying so much as a word, Luis disappeared into the home for several minutes. Men with megaphones passed by in pickup trucks, hawking crates of tangy tamarillo fruit. A few feet farther down the road from the house, the school, and the restaurant, I noticed a colorful mural under the shade of some trees that depicted a man, accompanied by two smiling donkeys, handing out books to children with outstretched arms.

The man from the mural came back out of the house just a few moments later, with two colorful wooden crates filled with stacks of children's picture books. He hung each one from the back seat of the motorcycle, and we were off once more, back down the road that brought me to La Gloria in the first place. I wondered how far we might be going—on the way here from Mompox, nearly an hour passed without a trace of much of anything at all, aside from a few clusters of farmhouses that were generously named as hamlets and were set amid the open, undulating pastures. But this was precisely Luis's point. Unlike in the Magdalena Medio, which rivaled this place in terms of emptiness, the names of most of the settlements here brought about a sense of hope. La Esperanza (Hope), El Paraíso (Paradise), and Nuevo Intento (Another Try) were a few. The one where we eventually stopped, about a mile down a dirt road turnoff along the highway, was called Santa Isabel. We reached a tiny farmhouse that overlooked some pasturelands populated by several dozen cows. This was where he kept Alfa and Beto nowadays, Luis said, since the roadside in La Gloria was getting too busy with trucks and cars for the animals to graze in peace.

Luis called out toward the farmhouse as we pulled up, and a farmhand came outside. He wore a very dirty Colombia national soccer team jersey proudly emblazoned with the name of Radamel Falcao, the country's longtime star striker. On his head, he had on a hat that said VENEZUELA. Luis greeted him with an emphatic handshake and a hug. They exchanged pleasantries before Luis looked at the man's hat and paused.

"Wait, are you Venezuelan?" he asked him.

The Venezuelan man laughed awkwardly, shrugging off the notion that he might be one of the million or so migrants seeking refuge in Colombia, but didn't say much after that. I could sense his embarrassment. He took us to a burro that was tied to a tree beside the farmhouse, staring blankly into space.

"Where is la burra?" Luis asked, and I realized that this one was Beto. "Could you go fetch her for me?"

"Well, I don't know …" The Venezuelan man trailed off.

"It's just that"—Luis leaned in and lowered his voice, so as not to offend the donkey—"this guy walks too fast."

The Venezuelan man pointed toward the pastures behind the house. "She's over there," he said. I looked and saw nothing but shrubs, some trees, and several dozen cows quietly grazing and minding their business. No donkey in sight.

"Ahhh." Luis nodded. Presumably he saw something that I did not see.

"She's over there?" I asked.

"Yes," Luis replied. "Over there." He pointed, very precisely, to the same vast expanse of green. I squinted and saw another cow.

Luis started walking back toward Beto, who was already at our disposal. "She's too far away," he continued. "It would take us too long to fetch her. We'll have to do with Beto on his own." Then he warned again, "But be careful, he walks very fast."

I understood and nodded. "It's no problem, I like to walk, I can catch up," I said. Luis smiled politely.

———

I WAS WRONG. WALKING ALONGSIDE BETO COULD VERY well be one of the more challenging tasks presented to a human being—not necessarily because he walks at the speed of light but because, as "Beto" and not "Alfa," he's used to following the leader . . . any leader. Usually, Luis brings only Alfa, or Alfa and Beto both. But today, Beto was alone and out of his comfort zone. Not used to leading, he felt inclined to follow someone, and that someone happened to be me.

Luis had harnessed the bookcases to Beto's saddle and mounted him for the trek out to some nearby homes. I was unable to walk anywhere else but directly in front of the animal, because he would follow precisely in my footsteps, imprinting on me as if I were Alfa or some mother goose. If I lagged behind or stopped to look at something, he, too, would stop and turn around. If I tried to sneak off to the side to take a photo, he would turn and walk toward me—even attempting to follow me up hills I'd climbed to gain a higher vantage point. Eventually, Luis got tired of this, I think, and he dismounted to lead Beto by a rope, freeing me of my leadership duties.

We stopped at one house along the way, after a few minutes, where Luis dropped off some books. But the children weren't there; instead, we were greeted by two men who emerged from the home and came to the front gate. Luis gave the men several books with specific instructions for their children, all of whom he mentioned by name. He emphasized that he was lending them the books to read and that they should finish them before he was to come around next, a few days from now. "I'll see you later, all right?" he said to them. "Take care of yourselves out here."

They nodded. "Gracias, Doctor," one of the men said.

I felt bad to see Luis walking, for the slight limp I'd noticed earlier had returned. I found this strange for a forty-six-year-old like him, who seemed to be in good physical shape, but I did not ask, just as I'd pretended not to notice Alejandra's forearm scar. At one point, we reached a large root that crossed the middle of the path, and Beto stepped gingerly over it. "Five years ago, I had an accident with Alfa and Beto," Luis said to me. He fell off of Alfa when she tripped on a log like this one, and one of the animals stepped on him. "My right leg split open, my bones were exposed, and I got a bad infection that forced the doctors to amputate." With help from various foundations who were aware of his work, he traveled to Georgia and Tennessee for the surgeries. He lifted up his pant leg slightly to show me a metal prosthetic. "I can't really get onto the donkeys so easily anymore, but I've gotten used to it now."

Luis told the story so gently, as if he were reading to a child. He always spoke like this. It took me a few moments to register the gravity of what had happened to him, to realize that it wasn't just part of the job.

In this way, we continued on our path, with not much else to do but walk and talk and watch the land. There is no true winter in Colombia, of course, only a wet season and a dry season, and everything is always green. A swarm of yellow butterflies fluttered up ahead of Luis and Beto, and I was once again reminded of *One Hundred Years of Solitude*, of the yellow butterflies that always preceded the arrival of Mauricio Babilonia, a character that represents all that there is to love in a world of struggle. The butterflies were native to the Magdalena Department, Luis said, where García Márquez grew up; their pastel wings were the same shade of yellow as the leaves of the cañaguate, Luis's favorite tree. "The most wonderful thing about being the Biblioburro is that you can get distracted by the natural world around you," Luis said. "I can tell you that I've seen up to three hundred birds on the most spectacular of days. You see butterflies of so many different colors, notice the behaviors of the insects . . .

"But the animals warn you of dangers, too. If you hear the woodpecker's constant screams, it's because there's someone hiding, watching what you're doing, or there's something unnatural in your midst. The woodpecker is an alarm."

This was especially useful all those years ago, when the paramilitaries were ever present, and kidnapping was a constant threat. Criminal groups often targeted and killed schoolteachers throughout Colombia, whom they accused of fostering subversion in future guerrillas through left-wing pedagogy in the classroom. It didn't help that Luis was such a prominent one. To get from one town to another, car travel used to be safe only in caravans. Soldiers were everywhere, but so were the bandits; they burned buses and killed and tortured ranchers, terrorizing villages like La Gloria. Once, riding through the countryside many years ago, Luis was tied to a tree by thieves. They stole just one book from his collection.

Luis told me about when a group of foreign reporters came to write a story about him. He was scared; it was 2008, one of the worst moments for security in the history of the Colombian countryside.

The reporters were accompanied by several members of the Colombian military as well as the police, who were monitoring the journalists round the clock at their hotel. "Total gringos," Luis said, and he laughed. They'd brought a translator and massive camera equipment that made them badly stick out. Though nothing happened to them, Luis's heart was racing all day.

"Is it still dangerous around here?" I asked. A question I'd been asking less and less since the chalupa docked in El Banco, but on the way out of Mompox earlier that morning, in the taxi, I'd heard a radio report saying that several infamous paramilitary men had been captured just blocks from where I was staying.

"Here the only risk left is the risk of wanting to stay." This was a common quip I'd heard many times along the length of the Magdalena when I asked if a place was dangerous, and I could never entirely figure out if it was true. But there didn't seem to be anyone for miles around, and Luis had a particular glimmer in his eye that made me want to believe him.

———

I SEEMED TO BE THE ONLY ONE WHO CALLED HIM LUIS. Doctor, Profe, Biblioburro. This was a man known by many names, and all of them were thrown around interchangeably by the large crowd that awaited us at the home of Berenice Díaz, after about an hour's walk through the savanna.

"They live without electricity," Luis whispered to me as we made our way toward the house, which sat atop a slight hill and consisted entirely of several tall, upright logs holding up a roof of palm fronds.

Berenice Díaz carried herself with a formidable matriarchal grace, presiding in a plastic-chair throne over the expansive hut that was their living room. It was completely exposed on every side, without any walls or flaps to keep out the wind or the rain (another equally large hut was farther away, in front of some eggplant, bean, and corn crops; I assumed that was where they slept, for it did have flaps, and more and more people kept emerging from it). A dozen of her family members—mainly sons and daughters, grandsons and granddaughters—sat around her, chatting with one another. One man napped in a hammock that hung between two of the logs that held up the roof. A brown-and-white dog lay silently on the hard dirt floor while she nursed five young at once. Berenice's husband, who looked much older than she did, offered Luis and me cups of sweet tinto, prepared with fresh sugarcane over a wood-burning stove in a large kitchen shack nearby. I could taste the coffee's smoky flavor as I sipped.

"We laughed the first time that we heard about a traveling library on a donkey," said one of Berenice's adult sons, "until we saw him coming down the road with his stack of books, notebooks, and pens, and he gathered the children, and the children stuck to him."

"When Juan Gossaín put him in the news on the radio, we laughed too, because we already had a front-row seat to all of it right here," Berenice added. "I said, 'Look where the Doctor is, he's in Bogotá collecting books to bring back for us.'"

"This is all wonderful," I said, "but where are the children?"

"I'll go fetch them," said one woman, and she stood up. A few minutes later, a young boy and a girl came out from behind the other hut. The girl was holding a six-month-old baby named Josué. They ran to Beto when they noticed him standing off in the shade, under some trees, waiting for Luis to follow. He did.

"Do you want to read a book?" Luis asked.

"Siii!" the girl, twelve years old, answered enthusiastically. The boy, who looked to be about ten, nodded silently in agreement.

Luis took out a book called *La cosa que más duele del mundo* (*The Thing That Hurts Most in the World*). "Because something has to hurt in this world, right?" Luis asked out loud while he was finding the book in Beto's load. The children didn't say anything to that.

"Once upon a time, there was a hyena and a hare that found themselves along the same river and decided to go fishing together." Luis read in Spanish to the children, who listened intently to his every word. "While they were fishing, the hare asked the hyena: 'Do you know what is the thing that hurts most in the world?'

"'The stomp of an elephant,' responded the hyena.

"'No!' said the hare.

"'A toothache.'

"'No!' the hare said again.

"'A wasp's sting.'

"'Not that either!'

"The hyena, tired of the game, said: 'I give up!'

"'The thing that hurts most in the world is lying,' answered the hare."

And on the story continued. Six-month-old Josué lost interest very quickly and started sucking his thumb. The boy and the girl were enthralled—the quiet boy especially, his eyes fixed on Luis, silently mesmerized. Beto stood patiently beside them.

Luis read aloud in a soothing, singsong voice—with a slow and almost musical cadence—rivaling that of any teacher I've ever had. It made me smile to think that there was now a network of nearly twenty Biblioburro traveling libraries, each operating separately throughout the Magdalena Department, doing precisely this at any given time. That in 2000, after his first three years with Alfa and Beto, Luis was able to open La Gloria's first primary school and permanent public library, now filled with computers and flat-screen televisions and piled high with books from around the world. Then he founded a second school, in an outlying village, and a third, and a fourth. Biblioburro itself has become a department-wide program, planning to roll out two new initiatives, Biblioburro Digital (bringing laptops, tablets, and other technologies to children in rural areas) and Biblioburro Very Well (a Biblioburro that teaches children English).

Later, I would also learn, not only did Biblioburro help the children, but it made Luis a better reader, too: "First I could only really read children's books myself, but now I like to read heavier literature, Colombian literature, postwar literature—books that make you think about things that are harder to grasp just from talking one person to another, but that you can get through storytelling." His bookshelves are filled with the thousands of donations he's received over the years, from *The Thing That Hurts Most in the World* to García Márquez's *One Hundred Years of Solitude* and Toni Morrison's *Home*.

———

WE SPENT SEVERAL MORE HOURS SITTING BENEATH THE palm fronds with Berenice and her family. As lunchtime neared, several other children trickled in from the fields, joining the tall girl, the shy boy, and six-month-old Josué, who was still sucking his thumb. They formed a circle around Luis, who knew all of their names, as he read several more books aloud. The dog on the floor continued to silently nurse her pups, and gray smoke continued to billow from the wooden kitchen. At times, Luis encouraged some of the older children to read to the others. One girl obliged. She read one page, to cheers and applause from the adults, before blushing and handing the book back to Luis.

"It makes me so satisfied to do this," Luis told me later. "And it makes me happy that my parents are proud of me." His parents, who'd emphasized education over all else, were now elderly—his mother eighty-two and his father eighty-six. They had watched their son grow up and defy all of the odds that were stacked against him from the moment he was born. But Luis Soriano is not a man who thinks only of himself. He notices everyone and everything around him: from the children, who read, to Alfa and Beto, who do the heavy lifting; from the sirirí bird, who sings, to García Márquez's yellow butterflies, who remind him of the beautiful leaves of his favorite cañaguate tree.

It was almost time for us to head back, for we'd already sweated through our shirts on the walk there, and the sun was only getting higher in the sky. I was chatting with the man who'd just awoken from his hammock nap when Luis looked up from gathering his things and tapped me on the shoulder. Signaling to me not to make a fuss about it, he pointed out the shy boy sitting a few feet away, at the edge of a plastic chair that was far too large for him, off to the side of the rest of the group. The boy had a book called *La mosca* (*The Fly*) in his hands and was mumbling the very same lines Luis had been reading out loud just minutes earlier. "'The great day has arrived,' said the fly," he read, quietly, to himself. "'It's time to take a bath . . .'" The beauty of the Biblioburro—what we were witnessing at that moment—was precisely what was missing when Luis was first a schoolteacher, all those years ago: that this boy, reserved and likely unconfident in his own abilities, would find it in him to pick up a book and start reading.

12

Mouths of Ash

UNTIL THEY CONSTRUCTED THE JETTY, BARRANQUILLA didn't have an eye toward the sea.

There used to be a delta, like that of the Mississippi, or the Nile—a sea of debris, tree trunks, flotsam from upriver. This was the Magdalena's final act of defiance before it absolved itself into the ocean: a place where, at any given time, one could find hints of recent events that had transpired farther upstream—trees felled, war victims left behind—recorded by the ever-present river and deposited, laid out for all to see, if anyone cared to look. But no one paid too much attention. All that seemed to matter was that ships couldn't pass the delta and reach Barranquilla straightaway. Instead, they had to go to Puerto Colombia, one hundred miles west along the coastline, where land was more accessible; there, the cargo and passengers would be hauled by train to Barranquilla, where they would then be placed onto Magdalena steamboats.

In the 1930s, the massive stone jetty was built to channelize the river, so that ships could easily enter the country straight from the sea. Workers laid a railroad track from the outskirts of Barranquilla to the start of the jetty and used a freight train to haul the boulders forward for its construction. As the jetty grew longer (two miles, three miles, four, five) the small train track was extended almost to the end. The whole thing was finished in 1936, thousands upon thousands of enormous boulders and stones piled up five miles long. Today, it's lined with huts and other small structures—places where people live, albeit tenuously. I still find it hard to comprehend how such a pile of rocks could suddenly just reroute a river and an ocean. And stay in its place.

———

THESE DAYS, THE LITTLE TRAIN LEFT FROM LAS FLORES, A sunny fishing neighborhood at the far northern reaches of Barranquilla with sandy lanes and pastel-colored houses. It reminded me of the motobalinera on steroids: a single vehicle that could be lifted on and off the tracks at will, not by one man but by five or six. Held up by the half dozen rail wheels was a metal platform, about the size of a small SUV, with benches facing each other the long way. The driver operated a pull-chain motor, like the ones on most wooden canoes, and at its best the apparatus probably reached twelve miles per hour, only slowly chugging along. Larger than the motobalinera, yes, but without the exhilaration of the ride.

"This stuff scares me." More a fan of boats than of makeshift trains, Germán Lozano was a marine biologist at the Universidad Simón Bolívar in Barranquilla, another friend of a friend who offered to accompany me, this time for the trip out to the point. With him, he brought his family—his wife, Oneida Guardiola, who worked in fisheries management, and his two teenage daughters—for this was supposed to be one of the most remarkable sights to see in Colombia. Though they were both technically my expert companions, they looked more like my parents. Germán was the quintessential dad, giddy with excitement for the day's adventure, and wore baggy cargo pants and large athletic sunglasses. Oneida offered me sunscreen. Their daughters hardly seemed as enthusiastic as we boarded the little train car at midday, complaining about the heat of the Caribbean sun that would fry us alive once we were out in the open.

The train left from a small restaurant at the edge of the wide, ash-colored Magdalena, nearly an ocean itself now, and proceeded due north toward the jetty. For a while, only the river was visible to our right, with trees to our left. Across the way, the land looked much prettier, even picturesque, with friendly palms swaying in the breeze. On our side, we passed many fishermen, some of whom used long tree branches as fishing poles and others of whom used coils of wire wrapped around tattered plastic bottles. I remembered twelve-year-old Gregory in Estación Cocorná, and his roll of string used for fishing and flying kites both. A number of long barges loaded with excavators and other construction machines lay dormant at the docks—I wondered if any of them would be setting off anytime soon, if the captain Álvaro Gulloso would soon see one beached along a sandy embankment near Gamarra or Vijagual from the window of his chalupa.

The train jolted as we reached the start of the jetty; on a GPS, it would have looked like we were floating away at sea, for naturally there shouldn't have been any land left. Yet we continued on the railroad track built into a bed of rocks. At times, it felt like the railcar was nearly the width of the entire jetty. To our left, where the thick trees had previously turned to dry mangroves, the dry mangroves gave way to an expanse of the shimmering blue Caribbean Sea. At first, it was calm, part of a protected bay, and people were bathing and refreshing themselves in its placid waters. Then we finally passed the sandbar that was holding it all together, and the sea unleashed its ferocity beside us.

I don't mean to suggest that the sea was any rougher than the river, really. There was a different kind of intense commotion on either side of the track: on the seaward side, it was a more organized violence, the long, arching, rhythmic blue waves pounding the rocks of the jetty; on the Magdalena side, it was utter chaos, the choppy, turbulent water appearing to flow in every possible direction as it neared its final destination. It was a spectacular sight, two thunderous bodies of water meeting, one a deep, inviting blue, and the other a stormy, ashen gray. I became jumpy at the thought of what it might look like when they finally came together.

————

FISHERMEN LIVED ON THE JETTY. AFTER ALMOST A MILE of nothing but a few tourist stands selling water and chips, we came upon their homes, a line of huts built from splintered wood and black tarps that stretched until just before the end.

"Look at their shirts," Oneida, the fisheries expert, whispered to me. "That man back there had a new shirt, nice and white." I looked back. She was gesturing toward a rather plump man with a clean, collared polo. He was holding a fishing rod with a shiny reel.

"Tourists," she continued. "That's how you can tell they're fishing for fun. Now look at *them*." She pointed at a group of sunbaked young men wearing clothes ragged and torn. They were fishing along a strip of ocean that was teeming with birds feeding at the surface, and pulling out one fish after the next, while another man just a few yards away had no birds in front of him and was coming up empty.

The train stopped at the end of the tracks, beside a statue of the Virgin Mary overlooking the remainder of the jetty that lay ahead, and we got off. It would be a one-hour scramble along slippery rocks and wooden planks to get to the end.

"Jordan." Germán ushered me over to one of the wooden shacks a bit farther up ahead. "Here, living so far away from everything, the fishermen are famous for their ingenious techniques."

"They fish with kites," Oneida clarified. They wanted to introduce me to a man they'd met in fishermen's association meetings in the city. He was known as the father of kite fishing in Colombia.

The man's name was Pompilio Ruiz, and he emerged from his home with a large roll of thick fishing wire in one hand and a kite in the other. He was in his fifties, shirtless, his skin peeling from the sun and salty air. His hair was curly, black, and wind battered.

The kite, built entirely from bamboo and plastic bags that were brought by the river and stranded on their rocks, was not nearly as elaborate as any of Alvarito's creations in Estación Cocorná. But it was incredible how quickly Pompilio lifted it into the air with the strong coastal wind. After a minute, it was hundreds of feet away, the string completely spent, and he made a quick move that was vital to the operation. He clipped the end of the kite string to the start of his long roll of fishing wire, which began with a plastic bottle a third of the way full. "To keep the hooks in the water," he clarified, and I still did not understand until I saw what he did next.

He let the bottle fly, to be carried away by the kite zooming in the wind. But all of the fishing line remained low to the water, held down by the weight of the bottle, and from it dangled seven smaller strings with baited hooks that dipped below the surface of the ocean. This was how Pompilio Ruiz presented his offerings each morning, and if he felt a bite, he would have to bring in the entire apparatus (including the kite) before unhooking the fish and sending it all back out again.

"Tarpon, mullet, shark . . ." He mentioned maybe a dozen species of saltwater fish he was accustomed to catching out here. I imagined him hauling in a reef shark or a tarpon longer than my arm from the end of his kite. The image I'd conjured up in my head seemed ridiculous, until a few minutes later, when another man holding a kite walked past, and hanging off of his backpack was a three-foot silver tarpon that was still heaving with the fading signs of life.

I wondered what life was like out here, forever exposed to the whipping wind and the beating rain, at the confluence of the Magdalena and the sea. Pompilio's house was a one-room shack; the dirt floors were littered with fishing equipment and various buckets that reeked of a mix of odors that included fish blood. He had a small wood-fired stove with just one pot, and a bed with torn, dirty sheets and a paper-thin mattress. He said that the first few hurricanes were scary, until the other men showed him that it was easy enough to rebuild. I noticed that many of the other homes here kept chickens. There were hardly any women or children.

"The men live here to fish," Oneida told me, "and many of them have their families in other places, like Las Flores, on the mainland." They spent most, if not all, of the days of the week out here on the jetty, fishing.

I asked Pompilio why everybody was only fishing the ocean side. "Well, some of the freshwater fish make it out here, but if they go too far toward the mouth of the river they die from the saltwater," he explained to me. "And then they're eaten by the fish in the sea. But yes, you get some bocachico, some bagre around." During certain months of the year, like January and February, when the river was drier upstream, it was most fishable here. But during all of the other months, it wasn't—there was just too much garbage and contamination brought by the deluge of water.

That seemed to be the theme, that this was the Magdalena's final dumping ground for all that it picked up in the country along the way. It was, after all, called Bocas de Ceniza, or "Mouths of Ash"— and it was like all the evidence of the fires burning inside the country were showing up here. "We used to see cadavers one after another after another," one of the older fishermen told me. "After a while, we stopped calling the police and just unsnagged them from the rocks ourselves." The jetty suffered from the thousands of plastic bottles and bags that were swept onto the rocks by the river, left to decompose over the course of an eternity—there were so many of them that I was tempted to think the jetty was built as much from trash now as it was from rocks. Plenty of material, at least, to build kites.

Near Pompilio's house we saw another man emerge from his

shack with a thick boa constrictor coiled around a heavy wooden stick. Another thing commonly brought to the jetty by the river. "It almost bit me!" the man announced.

"Constrictors don't bite, they *constrict*," Germán whispered to us, calling the man's bluff but curious to see what he would do next.

The man shook the snake onto the stone floor and used the stick to club it to death, smashing its face into a mess of blood and teeth— one of which stayed on the rock, he proudly showed another group of tourists. He tossed the bloody carcass back into the river, seemingly satisfied with what he had done.

I COULD FEEL THE SUN BURNING MY NECK AND THE BACKS of my ears. The heat all along the Magdalena felt never ending, yet forever changing. First there was the warm blanket of the rolling Andean hills, which came with the afternoon and went with the night; then, the inescapable, swampy heat of the lowlands that perpetually hovered over the earth; now, the heat was salty and stung with the spray of water and the whipping wind.

The girls didn't want to go on much farther than Pompilio's place, and Germán and Oneida decided that the four of them were going to stay back. I looked forward: about half a mile of rocks lay ahead of me until the point, which was marked by a signal tower that loomed large over us and the ocean on the other side. After a certain point, where the sandy path ended, I would have to scramble on all fours, jumping from boulder to boulder over gaps of gurgling seawater. My host family waved me off. I took a deep breath; for the first time along the Magdalena and in Colombia, nobody would be waiting for me when I arrived at my destination. I was on my own now.

I thought back to Abuelita Ana, Sandra's grandmother in Cali, from my very first visit; to Luis Manuel Salamanca in San Agustín, Doña Teresa and Felipe Ortiz in Girardot, and Isabel Romero's family in Estación Cocorná; to Alejandra Mayorca on the six-hour chalupa, and to Luis Soriano in La Gloria. Though I may have been traveling by myself, it so happened that in Colombia I was hardly ever alone: each of my encounters had led me to the next, all beginning with the sound of long and rambling piano melodies played by a woman whose life was filled with music. I also took to thinking about my ancestors, all those wandering merchants who could have found themselves on journeys as unfamiliar and interconnected as this one—about where they might have stopped, what they might have noticed, and which remnants of their experiences have trickled down through the generations to me. Traveling in this way, and trading in stories, is inevitably a journey of selection—it was not lost on me that for each voice I heard, many others would be left out. That each place I chose and every person I met would indelibly influence where I'd go next.

I started walking. Ten minutes . . . twenty minutes . . . thirty minutes. The looming cell tower didn't seem to be getting any closer, but the wind was picking up. I had to shield my eyes from it at times, it was so fierce, and I was rendered helpless to the tears that started streaming down my rippling cheeks. The ominous prophecy of Doña Juana in the highlands of the Andes echoed about: *The Laguna became enchanted and forever hostile to visitors.* For years, the prophecy felt true, not just at the Magdalena's headwaters but all the way to this grand river's end. Now, things are not so simple. A document may have been signed, but Colombia is not yet at peace with itself—that much became clear from traveling all along its greatest river, which cannot decide on one color as it ties together the ever-changing landscapes and peoples it passes along the way, and roils in its own turbulence as it exits a land of extreme beauty, burdens, and contradictions. There is as much work to be done to alleviate all the suffering war has left behind—for the communities mourning slaughtered activists, the families still displaced by lingering violence, and the species lost to quickening environmental degradation—as there are advances to be made in scientific discovery, in the availability of adequate education and social services for the most rural and vulnerable, and in the march toward justice for communities that have been marginalized for as long as they can remember.

It somewhat bothered me that a cell phone tower marked the end of the river's journey, and mine. But it felt fitting, too, this sense of subverted expectation—after all, I'd seen a country that defied common evocations and reminded me to look for megalithic statues in the mountains and colorful wooden canoes and filigree jewelers in towns with cobblestone streets.

The plastic bottles were a thick barrage now, and I found myself digging through them to get a handhold on the rocks. The end of the jetty was only for the most hardened of visitors. No one lived out here, but all the signs showed that some people came to fish. Small bones lay discarded on the rocks, which were brushed with flaky scales from days-old catches. I wondered how much the fishermen sold, and how much they ate themselves. I looked back to see if there was someone I could ask. The closest person seemed the size of my thumb. I looked forward again.

A cargo ship was approaching the mouth of the Magdalena from the open ocean, its freight preparing to start the long ride upriver. I scampered past the metal tower with all of the energy I had left, and hopped down onto the second-to-last boulder to finally catch a glimpse of the great show I'd come to witness. I sat, for the wind was so strong that I could not stand up. The end of the jetty is quite spectacular—the ashen river comes crashing into the blue sea with a ferocity that could rival the raging swells of the world's most famous shipwreck stories. The swells were ten feet high, and this loud clash of river and sea gave the water a distinctive brown hue, one I'd seen before—it was a rusty brown, almost like the color of coffee but also a dull gold. It was gold without shine or polish, but gold nonetheless.

At the end of the final rock in front of me, the last thing between the boulder and the sea, sat a solitary fisherman. He wore a wide-brimmed sombrero vueltiao and a neck gaiter to shield him from the sun, and a collared shirt and black rubber galoshes, too. He was generally safe from the crashing spray of the meeting of waters and meeting of worlds that lay ahead, and he seemed almost indifferent to the chaos swirling around him in every direction. He was focused on one thing: his kite, which he was using to fish. In his outstretched hands he held an old plastic bottle with a roll of wire that ran away from him, taut, into the air. You could tell that his eyes, though hidden by his sunglasses, were fixed on his contraption in the sky, which was glimmering and dancing in the wind and the sun. I turned to face it as well, which is when I noticed that while the man was alone, his kite was not. Beside it flew eight more kites, their strings each connecting them to other solitary men elsewhere along the jetty who might have been miles away.

Together, the kites danced above this magnificent confluence of sea and river and the Colombians of the frontier who faced it all. They didn't stop when I turned back and started walking again, or when we got to the little train and the little train pulled away and they faded from view. I like to think they're still up there now.

ACKNOWLEDGMENTS

THIS BOOK WOULD NOT EXIST WITHOUT THE HARD WORK, dedication, and generosity of so many people. My unwaveringly kind and supportive agent, Andrew Blauner, took a chance on me and has not lost faith for a moment since. I am very lucky to be working with an editor as brilliant as Megha Majumdar, whose thoughtful feedback and shared passion for travel writing as a vehicle for empathy and change touched this project in profound, innumerable ways. I cannot imagine this book in the world without Andrew and Megha, and I owe them both so much gratitude.

Working with the rest of the team at Catapult has been a dream. Thank you to Lexi Earle for creating such an epic cover, to Jordan Koluch for the beautiful book design, to Iza Wojciechowska for her precise copyedits, and to Rachel Fershleiser and Alisha Gorder for their enthusiasm and determination to bring this story to readers.

Before I knew it was to be a book, this project began while I was still a student at Princeton University. In addition to the generous university funding I received to carry out the reporting and research, I was privileged to learn from so many writers and professors whom I deeply admire. Christina Lee championed every aspect of this project, from when it was just an inkling of an unconventional thesis idea to the book that you hold in your hands today, and I don't know what I'd do without her guidance and wisdom. Thanks also to Daphne Kalotay, who first encouraged me to inject my own voice into this story, to make it more than just a collection of encounters. Pico Iyer has been the most incredible mentor in the world, introducing me to new ways of writing and traveling and thinking, and with so much care. John McPhee's course changed the way I see the world, and as a writer and a person, he has helped me find purpose. I will strive to follow his example with appreciation and admiration always. Joyce Carol Oates generously read early chapters, indeed my first writings ever on Colombia, and her encouragement kept me going. And during my thesis presentation, around graduation time, Jim Dwyer introduced himself and promptly offered to connect me with my now-agent—he went out of his way, and it changed my life. Read Jim's stories and you'll see that he was as good a person as they come; to him I will forever be indebted. So many others at Princeton—including Tom Dunne, Jamie Saxon, Mary Kemler, Margo Bresnen, Beth Heisler, and the team at Princeton ReachOut—were steadfast in their support of my work. My deepest thanks to all.

I am lucky to have made friendships along the Magdalena, and indeed all across Colombia, that I will always cherish. I hope that the deep gratitude I feel toward those who welcomed me into their lives and homes along the river has come through in these pages. Countless others supported this project behind the scenes, including Fernando Chaparro at the Universidad Nacional de Colombia, Humberto Sánchez at the Universidad Simón Bolívar, and Katherine Bonil Gómez at the Universidad del Norte; as well as the Wildlife Conservation Society, especially John Calvelli, Julie Kunen, Pato Salcedo, and Padu Franco, who gave me the chance to travel to Colombia in the first place. Sandra Cure Yunez, Miche Aleman Cure, and their entire family provided warm friendship and the most wonderful introductions across the Colombian Caribbean. Luis Alfredo Ceballos, a public librarian in San Agustín, is a dazzlingly brilliant reader, writer, and teacher whose passion for history and literature has inspired me every single step of the way. I honor the memories of Luis Manuel Salamanca of San Agustín, Simón Villanueva of Mompox, and Abuelita Ana Isabel Roa de Londoño of Cali, three gentle souls whose kindness I will never forget.

To Sandra Marlem Muñoz, who has graced my life with laughter and music for as long as I can remember, I'll forever be thankful.

I'm endlessly grateful to my friends, near and far, whose encouragement of my writing uplifts my spirits more than they will ever know. Special thanks to Ben Jacobson for reading countless early drafts of this and so much else with deep care and insight; and to Dan Sullivan, who somewhat unwittingly accompanied me on a bouncy Magdalena chalupa a year after my journey downriver, for his assistance with follow-up research, his dreams of adventure, and his friendship always.

My family deserves the final, and greatest, note of thanks. To my grandparents, aunts, and uncles, who laid the foundation for our lives in America and instilled in us their memories of the worlds they left behind: I tell these stories because of the stories you've told me. My brothers, Jonathan and Michael, are my best friends. And to my parents, I owe everything. I love you all.

FURTHER READING

Betancourt, Ingrid. *Even Silence Has an End: My Six Years of Captivity in the Colombian Jungle*. New York: Penguin Press, 2010.

Castelblanco-Martínez, D. N., R. A. Moreno-Arias, J. A. Velasco, J. W. Moreno-Bernal, S. Restrepo, E. A. Noguera-Urbano, M. P. Baptiste, L. M. García-Loaiza, and G. Jímenez. "A Hippo in the Room: Predicting the Persistence and Dispersion of an Invasive Mega-vertebrate in Colombia, South America." *Biological Conservation* 253 (January 2021).

Dávalos, Liliana M. "The San Lucas Mountain Range in Colombia: How Much Conservation Is Owed to the Violence?" *Biodiversity and Conservation* 10, no. 1 (2001), 69–78.

Davis, Wade. *Magdalena: River of Dreams*. New York: Knopf, 2020.

Drost, Nadja, prod. "N.N. (Ningún nombre)." *Radio Ambulante*,

April 17, 2013. Podcast, MP3 audio, 14:11. radioambulante.org /audio/nn.

Fals-Borda, Orlando. *Historia doble de la costa*. Bogotá: Carlos Valencia Editores, 1979.

García Márquez, Gabriel. "El río de la vida." *El País* (Madrid), March 24, 1981.

——. *The General in His Labyrinth*. Translated by Edith Grossman. New York: Knopf, 1990.

——. *Love in the Time of Cholera*. Translated by Edith Grossman. New York: Knopf, 1988.

——. *One Hundred Years of Solitude*. Translated by Gregory Rabassa. London: Jonathan Cape, 1970.

Giraldo, Juan Leonel. "Algunas gentes del río." In Noguera Mendoza, *Crónica grande*, 475–82.

Holton, Isaac. *New Granada: Twenty Months in the Andes*. New York: Harper and Brothers, 1857.

Jacobs, Michael. *The Robber of Memories: A River Journey through Colombia*. Berkeley, CA: Counterpoint, 2013.

Karl, Robert. *Forgotten Peace: Reform, Violence, and the Making of Contemporary Colombia*. Oakland: University of California Press, 2017.

Madiedo, Manuel María. "El boga del Magdalena." In Noguera Mendoza, *Crónica grande*, 511–15.

Niles, Blair. *Colombia: Land of Miracles*. New York: Century, 1924.

Noguera Mendoza, Aníbal, ed. *Crónica grande del Río de la Magdalena*. 2 vols. Bogotá: Ediciones Sol y Luz, 1980.

Reichel-Dolmatoff, Gerardo. *Colombia: Ancient People and Places*. London: Thames and Hudson, 1965.

————. *San Agustín: A Culture of Colombia*. London: Thames and Hudson, 1972.

Reyes, Luis Carlos. "Estimating the Causal Effect of Forced Eradication on Coca Cultivation in Colombian Municipalities." *World Development* 61 (September 2014), 70–84.

Rojas Bolaños, Omar Eduardo. *Ejecuciones extrajudiciales en Colombia, 2002–2010: Obediencia ciega en campos de batalla ficticios*. Bogotá: Ediciones USTA, 2017.

Röthlisberger, Ernst, and Miguel Cané. "Un viaje relatado dos veces." In Noguera Mendoza, *Crónica grande*, 187–202.

Suarez, Andrés, Paola Andrea Ârias-Arévalo, and Eliana Martínez-Mera. "Environmental Sustainability in Post-conflict Countries: Insights for Rural Colombia." *Environment, Development, and Sustainability* 20, no. 3 (2018), 997–1015.

Theroux, Paul. *The Old Patagonian Express: By Train through the Americas*. New York: Houghton Mifflin, 1979.

van Isschot, Louis. *The Social Origins of Human Rights: Protesting Political Violence in Colombia's Oil Capital, 1919–2010*. Madison: University of Wisconsin Press, 2015.

Vásquez, Juan Gabriel. *The Sound of Things Falling*. Translated by Anne McLean. New York: Riverhead, 2013.

Villamarín Pulido, Luis Alberto. *El ELN por dentro: Historia de la cuadrilla Carlos Alirio Buitrago*. Bogotá: Ediciones El Faraón, 1995.

© Nina Subin

JORDAN SALAMA's work has appeared in outlets including *The New York Times*, *National Geographic*, and *Scientific American*. A 2019 graduate of Princeton University, he lives in New York.